The Crafty Minx at Home

Also by Kelly Doust

*The Crafty Minx: creative recycling
and handmade treasures*

The Crafty Kid: projects for and with children

A Life in Frocks: a memoir

*Minxy Vintage: how to customise
and wear vintage clothing*

The Crafty Minx at Home

50+ handmade and
upcycled projects for
beautiful living

KELLY DOUST

HarperCollins*Publishers*

HarperCollins*Publishers*

First published in Australia in 2013
by HarperCollins*Publishers* Australia Pty Limited
ABN 36 009 913 517
harpercollins.com.au

HarperCollins*Publishers*

Level 13, 201 Elizabeth Street, Sydney NSW 2000, Australia
31 View Road, Glenfield, Auckland 0627, New Zealand
A 53, Sector 57, Noida, UP, India
77–85 Fulham Palace Road, London W6 8JB, United Kingdom
2 Bloor Street East, 20th floor, Toronto, Ontario M4W 1A8, Canada
10 East 53rd Street, New York NY 10022, USA

National Library of Australia Cataloguing-in-Publication entry:

Doust, Kelly.
 The crafty minx at home / Kelly Doust.
 ISBN: 978 0 7322 9657 5 (pbk.)
 Handicraft.
 Recycled products.
 Resourcefulness.
745.5

Cover and internal design by Jane Waterhouse, HarperCollins Design Studio
Photography by Amanda Prior Photography, amandaprior.com
Styling by Claire Delmar, clairedelmar.com.au
Cover and internal illustrations by Kristy Allen, pencilsessions.blogspot.com.au
Patterns illustrated by Kristy Allen, from original sketches by Georgina Bitcon
All other images by shutterstock.com
Colour reproduction by Graphic Print Group, Adelaide
Printed and bound in China by RR Donnelley on 157gsm Matt Art

5 4 3 2 1   13 14 15 16

For James & Olive

Foreword

One of the most interesting records of social change can be seen in furniture style and manufacture throughout the ages, speaking volumes about the wealth and taste of society in every period. Indeed, the current upcycling phenomenon is as accurate a reflection of our time as any other art form that exists. Because, while for generations our ancestors have been making do and mending with hand-me-down furniture, never before has there been such a movement created by the mix of anti-consumerism, thrift and a need to express oneself. As well as providing a visually pleasing way to furnish your nest, it also makes a strong social statement about the individual and one's place within the world.

The eclectic movement, which is currently entering into the mainstream (as style, more often than not, does), absolutely lends itself to the idea of the self as designer. Kelly Doust's book does not preach which approach you should conform to, but offers the know-how and inspiration to attempt many projects and adaptations to suit our own tastes. In this respect, it will stand the test of time, as good sense – as well as good taste – always prevails.

Although products of the now are often created from the inexpensive, discarded, unloved or outdated, the forces of consumerism are bound to kick in at some stage. Handcrafted and anti-mass-produced pieces will become as revered and collected as those from the turn of the last century. With renewed appreciation comes an elevated status of 'the rare'. This designer label effect is as interesting an observation on social change as the furniture we so dearly share our every waking moment with (and keenly judge each other by).

The 20th century spans many styles, many revivals of earlier periods and many discoveries of new materials and techniques; some as a reaction to excesses, and some as a necessity brought about by war or Board of Trade directives. But whereas wartime furniture was born out of shortage, the problem we face in the 21st century is the opposite: too much choice, and too many fads.

As a society, we're catching on relatively slowly to the absolute need to keep things out of landfill, but much is still being manufactured with intentionally short life spans. In years to come, it's likely we will look back on the beginning of the 21st century as a time when, as a global society, we turned this around and came to realise that surely enough is enough. We can pay

THE CRAFTY MINX AT HOME

homage to the past, but be mindful of the future by updating, recycling and mending these antique and vintage pieces as much as possible.

It has been a great pleasure to help with a few historical insights into various homely bits and pieces discussed in this book, and an honour to be asked to write the Foreword. As an auctioneer, it is heartwarming to be immersed in the world of the pre-loved, and the message of recycling and repurposing delivered in the pages ahead is shared in a delightful way. That said, Kelly does not preach frugalism, but more commonsense skills, to saving money when you can do-it-yourself, and spending precious pennies on the things you can't. This is the way to make your savings go further. The way you mix in designer purchases with homemade also says more about you than you think. Luckily, within these pages we have a guiding hand, and plenty of tips and tricks to make this more than achievable.

Revealing top tips for sourcing items, and ideas on the best things to collect, Kelly shares her useful advice on equipment and materials to help you on your upcycling adventures. This in itself is a great way to get started. Often we don't know why we buy oddments – we just know that one day they will be exactly what we're looking for. As confidence builds, so does the ability to visualise what we can do with a redundant item, and just a skerrick of imagination. Rather than adding to landfill with an old architect's table, how about repurposing that adjustable frame into a plasma screen holder? The ability to come up with these ideas is in all of us, and often the beauty of such pieces is in the simplicity of the ideas behind them.

I urge you to take up the advice given in *The Crafty Minx at Home*, and let your imagination be the only boundary. Whether you read avidly from cover to cover, or dip in and out for ideas in those all-too-rare quiet moments, it will provide the inspiration and guidance to tackle projects that will, in years to come, provide immense satisfaction: to you, your children and, hopefully, your grandchildren.

Shauna Farren-Price
Auctioneer and Valuer
Lawsons Auctioneer and Valuers, since 1884

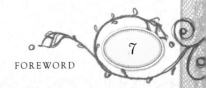

Contents

Introduction

$\mathscr{S}$imply put, I absolutely adore old things: old furniture and fabric, old homes, old clothes, old books, old recipes and old souls. I'm not an overly nostalgic person. I don't wish we lived in an earlier era and I embrace all modern advances that enhance my life. But objects laced with their own unique history tell so much more about the way we live. They murmur lost stories about the people who once handled them and the things they've seen, hinting at a secret life I find thrilling to imagine. This is also the element I appreciate most in a handmade object – the story behind its creation. A healthy dose of passion can be found in anything carefully made, and there's a certain kind of wisdom and authenticity that only comes with age. Both are something I find excuses to be around for their fascinating (and somewhat rare) charms.

My entrée into vintage style began as a teen with meagre funds I was looking to stretch further, and the discovery of local thrift stores. Starting with fashion, I branched out into homewares after moving into my first student share house, finding everything from Victorian bed frames,

Narnia-style armoires and ornate dressing tables, to cheery barkcloth curtains, lamps and hip '60s glassware to feather my adolescent nest. As I moved from one student home to another, I updated furniture and decoration to suit my needs and reflect my latest style crushes. I guess this is how most people start collecting vintage, although most usually stop when they can afford the new stuff. But for me, the allure of finding vintage treasure in other people's junk just increased. I still relish the challenge of sourcing unusual items I know no-one else can own or re-purpose in quite the same way. And no matter how much I have, I'm fairly certain I'll always decorate a room as well as I can on a limited budget. For a start, it means I can spend money on other things.

I can't think of one single brand-spanking-new item I've bought over the years that matches up to the hand-beaded '60s kaftan I wore so often over the course of a half-decade, it finally disintegrated at the seams before I turned its lovely bodice into a sofa cushion (which I still adore). It cost me twenty dollars at a local flea market, and always reminds me of nights out on the town, dancing till dawn, and the person I used to be. Or the hand-carved wooden cabinet I utilise to store all my crafting materials and (most of) my treasured vintage fabrics. Its scuffed surfaces show plentiful nicks and scratches from where its previous owner cut bread against the bare wood, and I can just imagine the work-worn hands of the man who made it. No new bathroom cabinet could ever beguile me the way those quirky old red-crossed medicine chests salvaged from hospitals do, and I cherish my re-upholstered '20s club lounge far more than is sensible. I have a feeling I will carry it to the grave, or at least put up a fight when I'm packed off to a nursing home without it.

Update your style more often, without making overly costly mistakes

Being thrifty is not the same as being cheap: it's about prioritising, and being clever and resourceful enough to invest in the things that matter most. When it comes to craft, the great tradition of thrift honours the skill and utility of vintage fabric, furniture or other items that are not quite ready to call it a day, and gives them a new lease of life. Embracing this trend not only makes good financial sense, but is environmentally sustainable. And it means you can update your style more often, without making overly costly mistakes. The French are big proponents of this process, with the best Gallic homes a display of this gradual 'life's work' process of home editing, which I like to think of as domestic curating.

Being either a vintage aficionado or devotee of new design is not mutually exclusive. Indeed, so many designers now re-work and rely upon classic styles to come up with their own take on vintage, that it's relatively easy to work thrifty items successfully into any modern home. Cherry-picking current designs and mixing them with older pieces actually works better, and is certainly more original, than having an interior decorator adopt a complete style for your home overnight, or more adventurous than working one look from floor to ceiling. Pairing a mid-century Danish sideboard, say, with this year's Mark Tuckey dining table and IKEA chairs is smart and achievable, and a design theory that stylists call 'high and low'.

Eclectic is now, and the most definable 'style' of the past decade is a trend likely to continue for some time. Our worldwide media culture means we're no longer influenced by local fads alone, or the imported curiosities brought along the old trade wind routes, but by everything across the globe. A mud-brick home in the African savannah, a feng shui'd Hong Kong penthouse or slick New York brownstones are all there at the click of a mouse, to voyeuristically peruse and be inspired by. This is both a blessing and a burden, because so much choice can be overwhelming. But emulate those ideas that really elicit a gut response, and you won't go wrong. Base your decorating concepts around styles that have always appealed, such as rooms spied in films, hotels you may have stayed in, or those conjured up by favourite novels. This can be incredibly fun.

Fashion a home that truly reflects who you are and nurtures all who live there

For example, one day I would love a bedroom to rival the colonial charm of the Sofitel Metropole in Vietnam's Hanoi, and my dream kitchen is straight out of *Moonstruck*; complete with subway tiles and Shaker-style cabinetry designed around a big farmhouse table for proper, passionate living. And maybe one day I'll have a decaying stately home like Miss Havisham's in *Great Expectations*.

To say vintage shopping is addictive is an understatement. Once you find that amazing, once-in-a-lifetime score – like the charming art deco-era Clarice Cliff plate marked at five dollars in a local charity store – it's all over. The bug has well and truly bit. After that it's an easy hop, skip and a jump away from scouring the auction houses and online dealers for bygone collectibles you've taken a shine to, or heading out at first light for lightning raids on flea markets and garage sales.

Modern crafting is almost indivisible from this appreciation of vintage and thrifting; all hark back to times where quality was prized over quantity – 'make do and mend', rather than 'grow bored and discard'. Forgive the lofty sentiment, but I think this growing desire for handmade, which goes far beyond designer labels and marketing spin, has a lot to do with people looking for authenticity in an increasingly inauthentic time in history. And an authentic home should be paramount: it's the place where we spend most of our lives – our natural habitat.

The spaces in which we live may be a kind of showcase, conveying what we want to show friends, family and occasionally the world at large, but a home designed for show is no home at all. Real, unique and personal should be the aim, containing a mixture of the things we love, use, have made ourselves or repurposed – or simply found in the right place at the

right time. Indulging in traditional crafts like sewing, woodwork, knitting or crochet, and developing an eye for pieces with integrity, is both achievable and fun, and injects your home with a style sensibility like no other. Above all, it's seriously fulfilling, and helps you fashion a home that truly reflects who you are and nurtures all who live there.

This book is broken down into different areas of the home to help inspire you to create for each room in a totally practical way, with lots of additional hints and tips. Some projects are almost embarrassingly simple, others are a little trickier and best attempted by the more ambitious or skilled crafter. There are also additional 'concept' sections, which aren't really projects at all, but more a collection of ideas and styling techniques to give you inspiration for looking at old items afresh, with an ample dash of prop trickery. And none of it would be complete without added information on some of the pieces mentioned, just to give our much-used domestic pieces an historical context, which is both fascinating and eccentric. I hope their stories surprise and delight you as much as they do me.

Creating a gorgeous living environment is a labour of love, and one that rewards tenfold what you put into it. Remember that, every time you're stitching or sanding or styling your way to true home happiness.

x Kelly

Shopping haunts

Spots for finding the best vintage pieces and reinvention materials

- ❦ Flea markets
- ❀ Charity stores
- ❦ Car boot sales
- ❀ Auction houses
- ❦ Antiques shops and centres boasting a selection of different stallholders
- ❀ Second-hand and bric-a-brac stores
- ❦ eBay
- ❀ Freecycling sites (search online to find items available in your area)
- ❦ Garage sales
- ❀ Hardware shops
- ❦ Haberdasheries
- ❀ Stationery and paper supplies stores

A Bit of Earth   Rebecca Smith

Top tips for sourcing vintage homewares and materials

🐝 Always try to devise a crafty solution for repairing, repurposing or totally reinventing vintage items, before you've forked over any money. Sometimes there's only so much surgery you can do and, if the job is too ambitious, it's highly likely you'll never get around to it. Don't be put off by dark or light wood stain, a bad paint job or unattractive lacquer on furniture – you can always sand pieces, such as armoires, dressing tables and chests of drawers, back to raw wood and coat with a pretty shade of matt paint, then rub in some beeswax or leftover scented candle wax for a softer effect. Paint designs such as cameos, curlicues, favourite motifs and stanzas in pretty script to add a personal touch. The same goes for damaged fabrics – read on for a plethora of hints and tips for fixing and re-working these to salvage the best repurposing materials.

🐝 Re-upholstering sofas and chairs can be expensive. Again, make sure the item you've chosen has a sturdy structure and desirable bones to begin with, before investing in new fabric or repairs. Generally, a shape that's gone out of fashion and come back in again (such as mid-century Danish furniture, wingback chairs and Chesterfield-style armchairs or sofas) will always be considered 'classic'.

🐝 Draft a rough list about what you like best, and keep those items in mind when rifling through markets, garage sales and job lots at auction houses. For example, I'm always on the lookout for any of the following items: quality damask tablecloths, hand-stitched linens, faded chintz fabrics from the '50s, commemorative tea towels, sturdy kitchen bowls, casserole dishes, enamelled pots and utensils in pleasing colours, English or Japanese bone china teacups, saucers and plates, old tea and biscuit tins with attractive dents and an authentic patina of age, tea cosies, cushions,

eiderdowns, unusual stools or chairs (particularly anything bentwood), Georgian or Victorian silver tea caddy sets, wicker picnic baskets, travel trunks and storage chests, tiny wooden children's chairs, flags, industrial hooks, metal lockers, old school desks and royalty memorabilia, to name but a few.

❧ Be patient and willing to rummage. The best bargains are always harder to find, and tend to come along when you're least expecting them. Shopping for quality vintage pieces is akin to a competitive sport at times, so if you're not willing to roll up your sleeves up and hunt through a whole lot of tat (while at the same time thinking in a highly creative way about its numerous possibilities) you're never going to find those really special pieces that some other canny shopper, stylist or boutique owner has overlooked.

❧ There's no shame in holding off until you find the object you've been searching for at an affordable price. Wait it out, if you have to. For example, I'm always scouring the UK auction sites for solid silver tea services and other silverware, but won't purchase when silver seems to be at its peak. Similarly, I often visit the chicest (read: most expensive) interiors stores in wealthy suburbs, but tend to hunt elsewhere for items I've spied there, rather than buying on the spot. More often than not, I'll find what I'm looking for at a fraction of the price.

❧ Go for outmoded or unpopular items and re-imagine them to fit your needs. When I started collecting mismatched teacups, saucers and plates they were cheaper than chips, because matching sets were *de rigueur*. I managed to amass a vast collection before the trend really caught on.

The same goes for cut glass and crystal, which had such nanna connotations for a while there, before they similarly rose in popularity. Trends come and go, but you'll score the best bargains with those pieces no-one else seems to be interested in. If you like it, go for it, and try not to pass up items you absolutely fall in love with or can't imagine living without. To paraphrase novelist Isabel Allende here, the only things I regret in life are the things I didn't buy.

- Look far afield. If you live in an urban, inner-city environment (particularly one located near a university or full of trendy people), you'll know that true bargains are few and far between. Try visiting charity shops and flea markets in country towns when you're on holiday, or those located in the outer suburbs of your area. And it's worth taking a day off mid-week to go op-shopping or auction house-trawling every once in a while. You'll be competing with dealers who snap up the best pieces to pass on at inflated prices, rather than all the other weekend shoppers like yourself.

- When in doubt, pair new with old, and high-end with low-rent. If you're unsure about how to work different vintage items together – a length of vintage fabric, buttons and lace, say – try pairing them with new pieces sourced from a gorgeous haberdashery, stationery or homewares store. This looks fresh and modern, and elevates relatively cheap materials to look more quirky or expensive.

- Consider filling old wardrobes or cupboards with space-age internal shelving and drawers rather than having built-ins installed. To my mind, collections of unusual freestanding pieces are so much more attractive, and still very useful storage-wise with creative internal reconfiguring. Try student stalwart IKEA or specialty storage shops. Oh, how I love those 'we live in 50m^2' signs above room set-ups in IKEA. Take note of how they manage to fit so much in; you might just learn a thing or two.

❦ If a second-hand piece is out of your price range, don't be afraid to bargain or ask if they offer a lay-by service. Bargaining is almost expected in flea markets, but don't be disrespectful: there's no need to point out all the flaws in an item or be rude to the stallholder. The way you ask is everything, so be nice and don't make an insulting offer. I bargain when I genuinely think something is too expensive or beyond my budget, and always do it in good humour. If someone likes you on the spot, they'll often find a way for you to buy it, even if it means putting it aside for you to return later or lowering their initial price. That said, bargaining in charity stores is a no-no. If it's really too expensive in that environment, just walk away.

❦ Take your vintage piece along when you're looking for materials to upgrade it. This takes the guesswork out of things, and allows you to seek a second opinion from store assistants if you feel you need it.

When in doubt, pair new with old, and high-end with low-rent

Sold, to the woman in red!
Canny auction tips and tricks

My friend Shauna Farren-Price has been working in the world of auction houses since 1992, so I defer to her on all things related to her industry. I asked her for the answers to some questions I thought auction novices would benefit from the most, and have included them here:

What's the best attitude to take with you to an auction house?

With a general sale, an open mind is a good starting point. There can be such a variety of things on sale that if you're too focused on getting that one particular item, you may overlook another. Take your time, and try to view on the day before the auction. Have a tape measure handy and know the dimensions of the wall or floor space you're trying to furnish. When you've done the preparation in a methodical way, carry this attitude through to the bidding stage and don't buy something on the spur of the moment that you haven't inspected previously. Just because something's selling for next to nothing does not a bargain make.

What should you look out for?

In all objects, I think the watchword is quality or craftsmanship. Something that is well made will be a sound investment, whether it's an antique or modern item. Open doors and pull drawers out to see how they fit together and slide. Check that the back of an object is finished as well as the front, and find out if the keys are available. If there's damage, check whether it's cosmetic or structural and assess whether a repair would be something you could tackle yourself. If not, don't forget to factor in restoration or re-upholstery costs. And check for signs of borer infestation (a pest that leaves pinprick holes and sawdust).

24

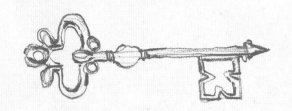

Which items will always fly off the auction house floor?

Large French farmhouse tables and pretty chandeliers, armoires, good Georgian dining room furniture, 1940s enamelled pendant lighting, stainless steel and timber workshop tables, as well as taxidermy and anything industrial. People like to throw a good dinner party and have something different to show off.

What are the things you would buy yourself, or think are great bargains?

It's not politically correct, but I would snap up fur coats by the dozen if I had somewhere to store or wear them. Costume jewellery is another product that sells by the bag-load and contains some interesting treasures. Other bargains include anything that can be cleverly repurposed, such as an old theodolite to be turned into a lamp, or a gunmetal architect's table used as a television stand. These will look amazing and unique in the right house. With art, sometimes the frame is more interesting than the painting and can be a work of art in its own right.

Can you share some of your best sourcing or bidding techniques?

Good sourcing is vital and can save hours. Most auction houses have online catalogues and newsletters, so you know what to expect before you visit, and a lot alert system, which takes the effort out of trawling through catalogues. Register a keyword wish list online, and receive an email alert when something matches your search. Always buy or download a catalogue to keep track of the sale. Ask the relevant specialist at the auction house for estimates on the item if they don't appear in the catalogue.

Most importantly, decide what something's worth to you and stick to it. Don't forget to factor in the buyer's premium, which is usually between 15 and 20%, and make sure you have a way of getting it home (this is particularly important for larger pieces). Most auction houses have a list of carriers or rental trucks to hand, but it's always best to check first.

Sometimes there will be two or more auctions running at once, which is tricky even for seasoned bidders. Work out the speed at which the auctioneer runs through the lots, so you can time your bidding and coffee breaks accordingly. Most general sales see about 90 lots an hour.

If you can't be in two places at once, make use of the absentee bid facility. Never hesitate to leave a bid because you think an item will go for much more than you're prepared to pay. I've missed out hundreds of times and always kick myself for not leaving a bid because I thought something would go for higher than I could manage. The auctioneer won't be offended by the sight of a cheeky bid listed on the book, although sometimes it produces a bit of mirth.

Other fripperies to collect and hoard

It's a delicious addiction to amass a veritable treasure trove of bits and pieces for adding unique flair to each item you overhaul, and I'm a fiend when it comes to these fancy fetish objects. Buy paints and threads in a rainbow of luscious hues for gorgeous contrasts, as well as vintage wallpaper, ribbons, buttons and trims galore. These items are often quite inexpensive to acquire and should be snapped up whenever you see them. Otherwise you might find yourself regretting it later, and returning to find they've disappeared, never to be found again (boo).

Here's a list of some of my favourite items to collect, almost ad infinitum:

- Sample pots of glossy or matt-finish acrylic paint in delicious gelato shades. A small collection (say, six to eight colours in 200ml (7fl oz) pots) is simple to acquire and provides a wonderful stash on hand for impromptu paint jobs. Take fabric or magazine images for reference on shades to your local hardware store, and match them up to colours they can mix for you.
- Neon spray paints – get your graffiti on. This is painting at its most fun and simple, even for the most impatient upcyclers.
- High-gloss acrylic paint or enamel in punchy brights, like scarlet, fuchsia, lime and Yves Klein blue (always great for brightening up the moment). Try a simple GT stripe on a boring chair or vintage suitcase and watch it POP.
- Vintage wallpaper, not just for walls. Use it to line the inside of a vintage travel trunk or decoupage a console, hall table or the back wall of a display case to spectacular effect. Metallic or velvet flock varieties look particularly fetching when put to this purpose.
- Vintage fruit crates, trunks, suitcases, wooden boxes or wicker baskets, which make quirky and brilliant storage for any room in the home.

- Tissue or crepe paper, as well as Japanese rice paper and origami sheets for delicate paper play.
- Pretty old postcards, cards or wrapping paper for unusual, nostalgic collage combinations with the aforementioned refined papers.
- Broken-down vintage atlases and coffee table-style books for decoupage.
- Remnant upholstery fabrics. Heavy-duty upholstery fabrics can cost a small fortune when cut from the bolt, so always ask for the remnant bin – you'll probably find large-enough off-cuts there for any number of individual home projects.
- Vintage fabrics salvaged from old curtains, tablecloths, tea towels or clothes. Use every available section by cutting around permanent stains or holes – even the tiniest scraps will find a use in handmade cards or delicate patch-up jobs.
- Chintzy, cross-stitched or embroidered hankies, napkins, tablecloths and tapestries for incorporating into modern quilts and all sorts of patchworked goodies.
- Too-ratty-to-wear 100% wool jumpers and cardigans for chopping up and reinventing as blankets, scarves, hot water bottle covers and soft toys for children.
- Oilcloth. Love, love this ingenious fabric, which is great for producing anything that needs to repel water or remain a little hardier (such as storage cases, tablecloths and bags). Mix and match polka dot, chintzy florals and nautical stripes for eclectic charm.
- Zippers in high-contrast shades, as well as old metal zippers with large teeth for injecting an authentic vintage vibe.
- Ceramic figurines – so cute and not at all nanna when given a modern twist, or placed in an otherwise uncluttered environment.
- 100% wool or silk yarns in every shade imaginable, and then some. I'm terribly acquisitive when it comes to yarns, often selecting favoured balls for display in bowls and baskets throughout winter to kickstart the incentive to create.

I like to think of this gradual life's
work process of home editing as
domestic curating

- ❦ Vintage frames salvaged from flea markets and thrift stores, in every size and shape imaginable. Old gilt versions with plentiful wooden curlicues are my favourite. Ignore the chips and paint over any damage with zingy brights.
- ❦ Patina-covered planters, vases, old jam jars and other unusual vessels for displaying crafty living displays, from windowsill herb gardens and posies to bedside terrariums.
- ❦ China or porcelain teacups and saucers for pretty storage, display and turning into candle-holders.
- ❦ Old grain sacks from health food stores – earthy, useful and quirkily printed for incorporating into otherwise simple patchwork projects.
- ❦ A selection of threads: black, white, beige and navy are the basics, but it's advisable to build up a vintage cookie tin full of colours for use on all fabrics. The general rule is to match thread to fabric (cotton for cotton, silk for silk and polyester or cotton polyester for synthetics) but cotton polyester threads are sturdy and work well on most fabrics. Colourwise, anything goes: use a contrasting colour if you want to highlight hems or a shade darker if you want it to blend in. A good tip is to wind half your bobbins with basic colours, so they're ready to use when needed.
- ❦ Pearl embroidery thread, also in a rainbow of colours: red, white, black, hot pink and electric blue are a great start for lovely contrasts.
- ❦ Fabrics of every colour, pattern, texture and weave under the sun – whatever grabs your fancy.
- ❦ Wool felt in candy colours, good enough to eat (yum).
- ❦ Calico and crunchy French linen neutrals for pattern-testing and pairing with prints and brights.
- ❦ Ribbons: Grosgrain and velvet are my particular favourites, but silk cord is also very useful for all manner of ribbon-related indulgences.
- ❦ Dried lavender or rose petals for scented sachets.
- ❦ Old keys, too pretty for the bin.
- ❦ Driftwood and shells.

- Buttons: I buy almost all of mine at flea markets and charity stores but eBay and Etsy are also a great pitstop for gorgeous vintage numbers in shell, horn, ivory, wood or ceramic. Lucky hunters will find old biscuit tins full of the beauties in thrift stores everywhere.
- Rickrack and other quirky, fabulous trims.
- Feathers and marabou trimmings (jazzy!).
- Sequins in every jewel tone and metallic shade imaginable.
- Beautiful glass beads of every description.
- Metallic threads for picking out a particularly pretty print or applying beads and sequins.
- Bias binding, especially the wider 25mm (1in) kind: find a gorgeous selection decorated with stripes, polka dots and cabbage rose-style florals in good haberdasheries, as well as the plain, single-toned kind.
- Interfacing and denim scraps: good for backing/stabilising delicate fabrics, such as shattered silks or organza.
- Broken jewellery: put aside any old jewellery or broken earrings and necklaces you might have, and hunt through boxes of mismatched items in flea markets – you never know when you might find a clever use for them and many items look great displayed on a pin board or sewn to handmade cards.
- Old chandelier crystals – I have quite a collection of these and am always adding to some sort of project or stringing them along fishing line to catch the light in a window.
- Pretty scraps of fabric, even if they're tiny and mostly trashed: silk, velvet and ditzy floral prints are great for covering moth holes, stains or tears with a luxe patch to add a handmade touch.

Homecoming

ENTRANCE AREAS TO
MAKE THE HEART SING

You only get one chance to make a first impression. Create an inspiring welcome area to draw friends in and set the scene, and exult in the feeling of relaxation that arrives when first stepping over the threshold of your home each day. Aim for calm and minimal, to project blessed peace, or layer the richest materials possible to create a cacophony of colour, texture and drama. Or simply let the play of light carry any message you wish to convey with a stark, decoration-free zone: the interiors version of a palate cleanser.

We all use our hallways in different ways, but it's also a useful place to discard mail, keys and umbrellas, for example, before we enter the home proper. For this reason, it's a good idea to incorporate utility into any styling ideas – after all, it needs to be liveable and practical as well as beautiful. Vintage pieces really come into their own here in the hall area in quirky, unusual ways. Consider using an old silver-plated toast rack to hold mail on a hall table, a hand-blown coloured-glass bowl for storing keys and spare change, or a pretty-yet-sturdy planter as an umbrella rack. Think inventively about the myriad ways in which items can be repurposed or upcycled.

Consider the people who will congregate in your hallway, and the impression you wish to create. Striking artworks, interesting curios picked up on your travels, treasured photographs, brightly threaded clothing displayed on hooks, and bold runners or furniture all make a statement about the personality of the people who live here. Make that message an encapsulation of all things unique to your family.

For the most significant settings, create a tableau infused with history: photographs of momentous occasions displayed in mismatched frames, moody images that speak of the home beyond, treasured books, or a stand-out item of furniture that demands attention and delivers maximum impact. And don't forget flowers in a quirky vase, or low-light options for evening. Nothing softens a space more than atmospheric blooms and flattering light.

Think of hallways as the most-frequented room of your home, and decorate accordingly. Make it attractive, not too serious, and heaped very generously with love.

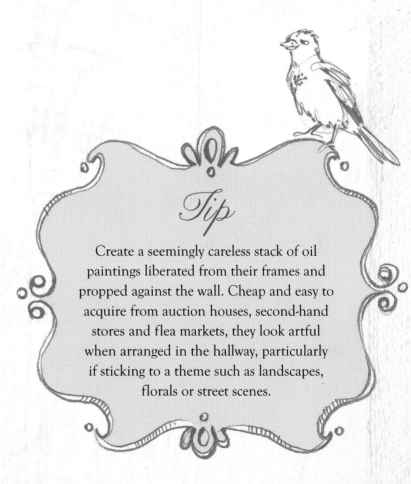

Tip

Create a seemingly careless stack of oil paintings liberated from their frames and propped against the wall. Cheap and easy to acquire from auction houses, second-hand stores and flea markets, they look artful when arranged in the hallway, particularly if sticking to a theme such as landscapes, florals or street scenes.

You can leave your hat on
beribboned coat stand

I love the organised chaos of a coat stand displaying favourite coats, scarves, totes and hats, positioned near the front door. With a little tweaking for artistic effect, a brightly adorned stand creates a charming focal point to the entrance area or hallway, and shares a few secrets about the character of the people who live here.

Forget your standard black caps and coats: display kooky hats, kimonos and favourite dress-up items for frivolous effect.

Bentwood coat stands are a dying breed, but they can be snapped up for a song in second-hand furniture stores and flea markets and look beautiful painted neon orange, pink or yellow, or wrapped in a fetching array of ribbons and torn fabric. In the absence of pretty wooden versions, find an old metal frame and wrap tightly with rolls of ribbon in gorgeous hues instead.

MATERIALS NEEDED

- A second-hand coat stand
- Rolls of bright ribbon, enough to cover entire stand in lovely contrasting designs
- Masking tape
- Scissors
- Drawing pins

INSTRUCTIONS

1. Starting at the base of the coat stand, attach the end of your ribbon roll with a piece of masking tape and begin the process of winding it around one foot, making sure to cover the masking tape with ribbon first.

2. Work your way upwards, continuing to wind the ribbon neatly until you reach the top of the foot. Wind a little way up the centre pole, then snip off unnecessary ribbon and tape into place.

3. Repeat the above two steps for the second foot, making sure the ribbon covering the base of the pole is not too bulky (remove tape and snip some off if you need to).

4. When you get to the third or fourth foot, follow the same steps above, but keep winding the ribbon up the pole after covering the spot where the ribbon from each foot meets. Continue winding upwards around the pole. When you cannot hide masking tape with ribbon, use a drawing pin to secure in place. Simply fold over the end and tuck underneath before pinning to hide its raw edge.

5. When you reach the top hooks, wind ribbon around one hook until you reach its tip, then snip off any excess, tucking under the raw edge and winding back on itself before securing with a drawing pin.

6. For the remaining hooks, tape end of ribbon length into place near the pole, then wind ribbon downwards to cover any gap before winding upwards again towards each tip. Snip off any excess, tuck under the raw edge and secure in place with drawing pins.

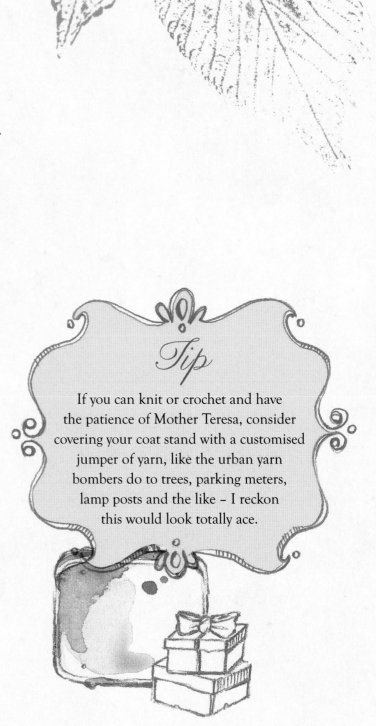

Tip

If you can knit or crochet and have the patience of Mother Teresa, consider covering your coat stand with a customised jumper of yarn, like the urban yarn bombers do to trees, parking meters, lamp posts and the like – I reckon this would look totally ace.

THE CRAFTY MINX AT HOME

COAT STAND + HALL TABLE = HALLSTAND

The hallstand is one piece of furniture that has truly changed with the times, not only stylistically, but in terms of utility. One of the most important pieces of furniture in the modern era, it is usually the first thing we reach for when we arrive home, or the last thing we check before leaving the house. If ever a piece of furniture could signify the distinction between home and away, it's the hallstand. A receptacle for mail, all manner of clothing, keys, mobile phones, Post-It notes and scribbled instructions to put out the cat or buy milk, this is one clever multi-tasker that has been seen in many guises since its humble beginnings as a basic table married to a coat stand.

The design for the coat stand stems from the late Georgian, and particularly Regency, period, a time when the popularity of social visiting and clothing fashions rose in equal measure. By the mid-1850s, Gebrüder Thonet had developed the quintessential coat rack for Cafe Daum, one of the most famous cafes in Viennese history, frequented as it was by politicians and important military personnel. Still in production more than 160 years later, there has been little change to its design and production since. Its basic layering of bentwood forms the curves for hanging and stability, which give it such timeless appeal.

During the Victorian era, they began to incorporate mirrors, tabletops, a drawer, pegs and hooks, receptacles for umbrellas, walking sticks and, often, a shelf atop or cupboard below in the hall stand. Larger versions would feature a built-in, hinged seat and hunting lodges had similar pieces built with horns and antlers for somewhat macabre hooks.

Elegant tableau
decoupage hall table

One of those folksy crafts that look naff when done badly (think cupid-covered jewellery or hat boxes), decoupage is an amazing skill to develop properly. If visiting the buzzing village workshops of Vietnam, you can see for yourself how the craft has been developed into a high art form, using delicate gold leaf and miniscule shards of broken eggshell to spectacular effect. The traditionally lacquered and elegant bird and flower imagery looks simply magnificent unfurled across rosewood or teak furniture: a fine skill, which has come to be appreciated the world over.

The trick for artful decoupage is to combine beautiful paper with a well-formed item of furniture, and complete the entire process with care. Patience isn't one of my strong suits, but I'll spend a good deal of time laying out imagery just to make sure it all fits together and looks pleasing, well before I start in with the glue. Painting on lacquer takes careful consideration, too, if you want to avoid that tacky, stuck-on effect.

Search out a console or side table fit for this purpose at a flea market or second-hand furniture store. Assess its height and sturdiness for holding mail, a vase of flowers or table lamp (drawers also prove handy for messy items, such as keys, loose change and spare bits and bobs), and disregard any nicks or scratches, because they're about to be covered up. You're now ready to begin.

Combine beautiful paper
with well-formed furniture
for artful decoupage

THE CRAFTY MINX *AT HOME*

MATERIALS NEEDED

- Item of furniture, such as this wooden hall table
- Scraps of pretty paper and images – mine have been chopped out from last year's wall calendar and various greeting cards with a small, sharp set of scissors for precision. I have also used a length of vintage wallpaper
- Digital camera or phone with camera feature
- Sandpaper and block
- Cloth
- Decoupage glue (or PVA glue mixed 3:1 with water)
- Ruler or rubber roller
- Clear lacquer or varnish
- Paintbrush

INSTRUCTIONS

1 Take all your pieces of decorative paper and lay them out over the surface of your hall table until you're happy with the results. Snap a digital image to remind yourself where you'd like each piece to sit.

2 Sand back the wooden surface on your table, and remove all dust with a damp cloth until completely smooth.

3 Apply glue to the surface of your table, then place the decorative pieces into position. (It is safer to apply glue to the table surface rather than to the back of the paper, since you might tear or stretch the paper.) Paint over more glue, while at the same time working any bubbles to the edges. Smooth surfaces down flat, gently using a ruler or rubber roller, to avoid air bubbles forming between the surface and paper. Wipe over with a damp cloth to remove any excess glue and leave to dry.

4 When the glue is completely dry, carefully paint over the entire piece of furniture with six to eight coats of clear lacquer, allowing each coat to dry completely before applying the next. Avoid obvious brush strokes, and eradicate any thicker, coagulating blobs with a damp cloth or by using small, even brush strokes to smooth any drips. This gives your table a lovely even surface.

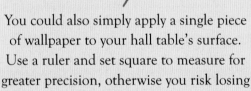

Tip

You could also simply apply a single piece of wallpaper to your hall table's surface. Use a ruler and set square to measure for greater precision, otherwise you risk losing a more professional-looking finish. Metallic wallpapers look particularly luxe with this treatment, almost as though they were painted directly onto its surface.

The lamp shown here is a rare French antique, which was a candelabra in its first incarnation. With chandelier crystals and unusual finial (the ornate 'hero' crystal at its centre) it's been wired to bulbs where the candles were once inserted. Rusty and covered in dust, with many of the crystals coming away from the metal when I found it, I've lovingly polished up each crystal and used a length of similarly rusted wire to attach them back into place. I don't mind the patina of rust, and adore the quality of light it casts with its candle-shaped bulbs and glittering crystals. About a century old, it should last another century or more in its new guise.

Let there be light
antique-something-turned-lamp

While on your travels, always keep eyes peeled for unusual lamp bases or appropriately shaped items that could be wired to create a unique statement lamp.

It's a favourite daily ritual of mine to prowl through the house in the half-light of dusk, turning on the lamps in each room, in preparation for evening. We use the overhead fixtures only once in a blue moon because, in our house, it's all about the lamps; not only does great lighting create a moody atmosphere (cosy and welcoming or stark and dramatic, for example) but life's simply better lived in flattering light.

I like the clean lines of modern lamps well enough, but one in every room can be boring – that's why I like to mix with older versions, or left-of-centre items people wouldn't normally consider repurposing as bases. If you fall in love with an appropriate piece, it's worth the investment to have it turned into a lamp by an electrician or lighting specialist. Vintage vases make fantastically quirky lamp bases, as do ceramic figurines, metal industrial scraps and wooden sculptures. You just need someone capable of making the transformation. It's a job I leave to the professionals, but simple wiring is possible with a kit picked up from your local hardware or lighting store.

Life's simply better lived in flattering light

CUSTOMISATION AND REPAIR IDEAS

❦ Consult an electrician or lighting specialist to have your antique-something reinvented as a lamp base, or make a trip to your local hardware and enquire about re-wiring kits. You may need to use a drill to help thread through the wires, or you could attach to the back of the base with staples, hidden from view.

❦ For plain vases with interesting shapes, consider painting a unique pattern directly onto the ceramic with paint and a layer of matt lacquer to seal.

❦ Banish uglier patches of rust with oil or rust remover, but leave an authentic, attractive patina of age.

❦ Pair the base with a modern shade, or cover a dusty, damaged old shade with a new layer of fabric or wallpaper.

THINGS YOU MIGHT NEED TO CUSTOMISE AND REPAIR YOUR ANTIQUE-SOMETHING

- Original antique candelabra, vase or interesting sculpture find
- Electrical re-wiring kit
- Drill
- Staple gun and staples
- Rust remover or oil / glass cleaner and cloth
- Thin garden wire (left outside to rust if need be, to match old wires already in place)
- Ceramic paint, to gussy up a plain vase, and matt lacquer

Tip

Vintage and retro lamp bases are so easy to find in markets and second-hand stores. As a rule of thumb, pair sleek shades with a kooky base, or unusual shades with an industrial or plain-looking base. This creates interesting, out-of-the-ordinary contrasts.

House of chairs
upholstered vintage stool

Why house of chairs? Because I love vintage chairs so very much – all chairs, really – I could fill an entire home with them. It takes a mighty amount of willpower to step away from classic wishbone, butterfly or bentwood styles, not to mention plush armchairs, pews, dainty dressing table stools and rustic wooden milking props when I find them. I won't try deciphering the beginning of this obsession, but perhaps it's something to do with the idea that a room without chairs has no space for rest at all, and surely every room needs ample resting place?

A humble wooden chair, such as the old schoolhouse style shown overleaf, is much improved with a coat of paint and vintage fabric-covered cushion. Place in the hallway for a moment of respite before entering the home proper, or decorate with discarded panama and a favourite hardback or two for a chic still life.

Collect lengths of beautiful '50s upholstery fabric, such as the pretty, chintzy linen I've used (most likely intended for making a dress or curtains), and paint your piece in a fresh or striking tone to match.

MATERIALS NEEDED

- Old wooden chair or stool
- Sanding block and cloth
- Matt paint – a sample pot should be enough to cover an entire chair with a few coats
- Paintbrush
- Vintage fabric – thicker upholstery fabrics, such as barkcloth and heavy linen work best
- Foam cushion or base – use a pre-bought cushion or purchase from a specialist foam supplier
- Staple gun
- Scissors

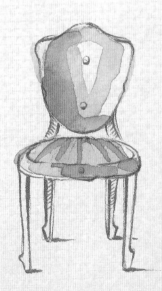

49

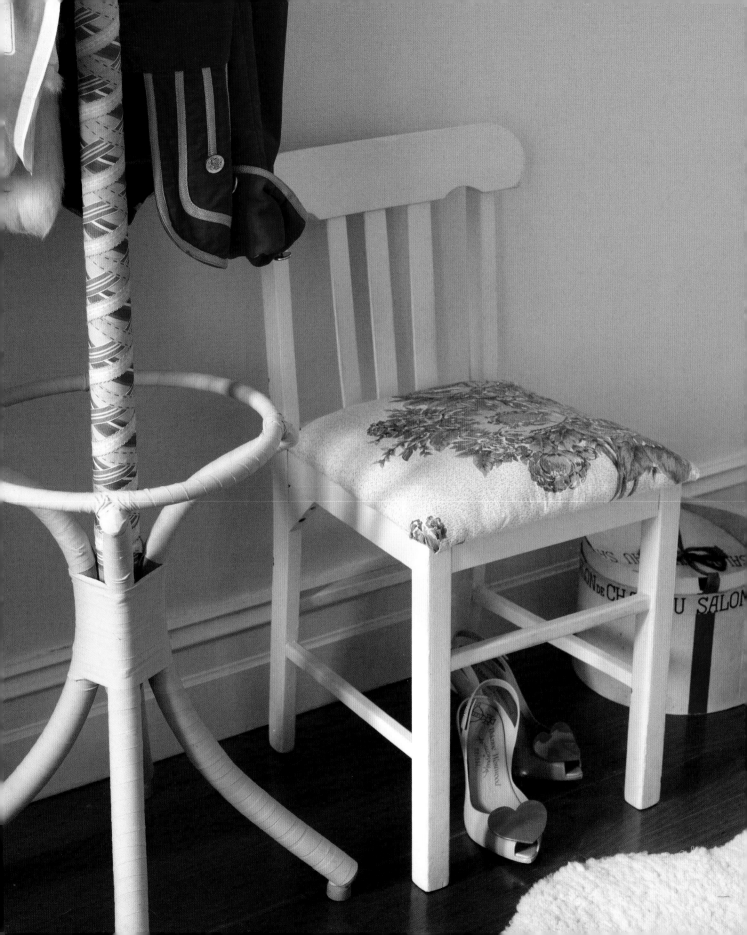

INSTRUCTIONS

1. Sand off any rough edges on your vintage wooden chair, and remove dust with a damp cloth.

2. Paint your chair with a few coats of dusty-effect matt paint in a shade you adore, such as this pale, candy-coloured pink, lemon, duck-egg blue or spearmint green (all tones which are very '50s in flavour).

3. Take your foam base or cushion and place in the middle of the seat. Cover with fabric to work out exactly how much will be needed to wrap over the stool and underneath, leaving a few centimetres (an inch) or so spare to fold under any raw edges.

4. Cut around all four sides or around the circular seat.

5. Roll under the raw edges, pull into place, and start stapling fabric directly to the underside of the chair – you might need an extra set of hands to keep things firmly in place while doing so. If you're covering a chair that has a back, rather than a stool, fold under the fabric and staple very close to the wrapped foam edge so the staples are virtually invisible. Or use a hammer and Chesterfield-style upholstery pins (available from a hardware store or upholsterers) to secure fabric at the back of the chair.

BENTWOOD LOVE

In 1859, German-Austrian furniture maker Thonet (pronounced TAWN-at) created the 'Konsumstuhl Nr. 14' or Coffee Shop Chair No. 14. Constructed from wood, heated and bent by steam technology, it still remains one of the best-selling chairs ever designed. Made from six pieces of steam-bent wood, ten screws and two nuts, the sensuously curvaceous chair is relatively easily to construct and take apart, with a seat often made from woven cane or palm (chosen because the holes let spilt liquid drain off easily – ingeniously useful in a café environment).

At the Paris World Fair in 1867, the bentwood chair won a gold medal and sold 15 million pieces between 1860 and 1930 alone.

Ode to good living

SPECIAL SITTING ROOMS

*W*hy else would they commonly be referred to as 'living' rooms? The sitting room is a room for life, and all that this involves: a place to unwind with family, relish a few moments in your own company, read, watch films, entertain friends or turn your hand to gentle crafts. Where we congregate with friends in the most relaxed of ways, play with our children, and share time.

The sitting room is the most versatile room of the home and, of all its spaces, needs re-styling often to avoid becoming stale. Reflect fresh energy with newly plucked flowers and frequently changing art, furniture placement and floor coverings. Plus a decent stereo for playing ambient tunes. We have lovely polished floorboards in ours, so every summer I roll away the plush wool rug (so soft underfoot in winter) to reveal bare boards, save for a single sheepskin in case someone fancies a spell on the floor. The artworks and soft furnishings also revolve and change; in summer pale shades dominate for a bright, breezy feel, finding themselves replaced in winter with warmer textures and colours overall. Start with cushions for a makeover, and create a new mood altogether with crafted displays or complementary plants. Potted orchids are a winner all year round, in cymbidium-white or rich burgundies. For dark wood furniture, surfaces may be covered with pale runners and throws in summer, or left bare in winter for womb-like warmth.

When a television dominates, sitting rooms feel more utilitarian than social. Try placing yours off to the side or mounting it on the wall so at least a sofa and chair face each other. Opposing sofas create a cosy, convivial environment.

For tiny spaces, consider going without a coffee table and using side tables instead, so this sort of formation is possible. Create artful clusters of light in the form of table lamps, candlesticks and reflective mirrors, which create such a warm, welcoming atmosphere and beat overhead lights (hands-down) for gorgeous ambience.

In my ideal sitting room, there would be two sofas, an angle-poise floor lamp placed nearby for reading, a huge floor-to-ceiling bookshelf, coffee table, side tables, armchair and table lamps placed strategically for versatile lighting effects. Not to mention a gallery of art on the walls surrounding a beautiful mantelpiece and open fire (the hearth still being the best focal point for any sitting room, even after centuries of household evolution).

If you spend more time entertaining in the kitchen or dining room, try moving the action to the sitting room once in a while for a shift in temperament. Intimate rooms invite intimacy, so it's the perfect space for conversation. And creativity: try a high tea celebration with a group of girlfriends, invite friends' children over for a birthday party or conduct an old-fashioned quilting or knitting bee. Layer the memories for a sitting room with heart and feel the way it nurtures, year after year.

Curl up
spectacular sofas

A perfect sofa is that one-off purchase to make when you're a fully fledged adult, with your own home and income. Chosen well, it should see you through myriad style incarnations over the course of a lifetime, and acquire a perfectly lived-in, loved-in look, without tipping over into looking grungy.

For my money, vintage pieces win every time over new sofas or armchairs. Not only do they add character to any home, but your accountant will appreciate the thrifty sentiment; the vast majority of vintage or retro pieces cost far less than new (and often less well-made) versions on offer, even with a fancy upgrade. Put aside squeamishness over old fabric and fillings, which are easy – and relatively cheap – to replace.

Tips for acquiring your perfect vintage sofa

❦ First up, you need to know where to look. I'd probably try an auction house if I were looking to invest in an old/new sofa, but eBay, second-hand stores, charity shops, garage sales and antiques dealers are also an excellent source of quality sofa sets and armchairs. Remember, you pay a premium at antiques centres or well-edited stores located in fancy areas. For the best bargains, be willing to rummage in the less-salubrious parts of town.

❦ Find a decent upholsterer or consider undertaking the project yourself. I'll turn my hand to simple upholstery for a chair seat or outdoor setting, but tend to leave proper upholstery work on big-ticket items to the professionals. Ask around for recommendations. Good fabric stores will often pass on their list of preferred upholsterers. Ask to see pictures of previous work, and visit their workshop so you know what to expect. Compare quotes: these can vary wildly, and are often dependent upon how much the upholsterer wants your business.

PROTEST

Balance the beautiful with the practical

Hark at my '20s club lounge and two
matching armchairs: I bought the lot for
$100 from an auction house, and had
them completely refurbished with new
padding, upholstery and a fetching French
polish. Even with all this work, the charm
of the original pieces still remains.

❧ Look to old pieces with beautiful, classic bone structure. Ignore ugly or damaged upholstery and scratches on wooden arms or legs: these can be fixed with a new set of threads and cleverly applied French polish. Danish-designed or replica mid-century furniture is super-covetable and quite readily available second-hand. As are plush, down-filled '70s-era pieces in any shade of brown and threadbare '50s numbers, which tend to be much less expensive. My preference is for '20s-era club lounges: the low-slung, rounded style just oozes the vibe of low-lit speakeasies and the golden jazz age.

❧ Choose fabric you've fallen in love with, or one that is completely neutral. I initially pined for eggshell damask or pale blue velvet for my club sofa, but ended up choosing this hard-wearing design instead, which is unlikely to date or become too grubby anytime soon.

Tip

Items properly referred to as antique were made prior to the 1920s. True vintage pieces are from the '20s through to the '60s eras, retro is '70s or '80s, and anything from the '90s or more recent times is simply second-hand.

Tip

French polishing works a treat for sprucing up tired-looking wooden furniture, but try this natural solution for disguising small dings and scratches: rub them with a walnut. It works!

THE SOFA IS BORN

After many millenia of lavishly decorated timber pieces (and once the privilege of church and monarchy, the ruling classes) chairs became attainable to wealthy landowners around the 17th century. Upholstered by specialist craftsmen in increasingly lavish ways, it's thought this development was initially to hide the timber frames and complement tapestries on the walls of stately homes, rather than out of any great need for comfort. Since then, shapes and sizes have steadily changed over the years to accommodate fashions of the day, such as wider chairs with shorter arms which enabled sitters to wear voluminous frocks with bustles and a whole lot of hoop(la) in the underwear department without getting stuck.

After years of sitting on hard timber benches, sofas were then developed as a comfortable alternative and usually stuffed with hog or horsehair on jute webbing. Early examples that have survived in some numbers are the Georgian camel back sofas from about the 1770s, so called because of a characteristic hump at the back. Earlier still, in terms of design, are the Knole settees or sofas, which originated in the 17th century and were named after the now National Trust-owned Knole house in Sevenoaks, Kent. The design features a back and hinged arms or sides that are the same height, often with beautifully carved wooden finials and ends tied together with heavy braids and tassels.

The Victorians and Edwardians loved a good parlour suite, often comprising settees, chairs, armchairs and chaises. The usual formation was a five- or seven-piece matching suite with carved timber frames. Moving on to the art deco period in between the wars, the suite developed into a more comfortable, overstuffed and fully-upholstered setting, more akin to the typical three-piece suites we're familiar with. Now in the 21st century, mix and match trends are *de rigueur*, with the three-piece waning in popularity.

Total comeback vintage cushions

So you love the quirky designs seen on retro cushions, but they're threadbare or damaged and, quite frankly, you're afraid of where they've been? Me too. The thought of dust mites and moths is enough to give one the heebie jeebies, but it shouldn't put you off collecting old cushions to adorn your home. A charming new cushion or three is the simplest way to update a staid room, and what could be better than showcasing a print or two no-one else seems to own to make your space even more unique?

INSTRUCTIONS FOR REINVENTING VINTAGE CUSHIONS

1 The first thing I tend to do with musty old cushions made from fabrics worth saving is to unpick the bottom hem, or make a slit with scissors, and scoop out all the old stuffing (unless it has a zip, in which case simply remove the cushion). Whether it's feathers, wool or polyester filling, this all goes in the bin.

2 Pop the cushion cover in a plastic bag, tie a knot and chuck in the freezer for 24 hours to kill off any moth eggs or nasties. Remove, put through a hot cycle in the washing machine (unless it's very fragile) and dry in the sun.

3 For bad stains, soak in nappy cleaning solution and dry outside on a sunny day, without washing out the detergent first. Most stains will fade or disappear but be warned, it may also fade fabric (be extra careful with silk or velvet, and wash by hand).

4 If you're left with persistent stains or holes, embellish over them with sequins or pearl embroidery thread, or cover with fabric yoyos (see instructions for how to make these on page 62).

5 Add a contrasting ruffle around the outside (for instructions, see page 62).

6 Find a new cushion to fill the case, or stuff with wool or polyester filling before stitching closed. Throw on the sofa and admire your cleverly thrifted collection.

Vintage cushions are inexpensive
in charity stores and flea markets.
The '40s-era birds and '50s-era chintz
cushions shown here cost only a few
dollars apiece, and very little more
to update.

INSTRUCTIONS FOR CREATING YOYOS

1. Using a saucer or wine glass rim as your 'pattern', trace around the outside circle with dressmakers' chalk before cutting out your circles (or use a special yoyo maker, which is cheap and readily available at good haberdasheries).

2. To make each yoyo, fold over the circle's edge by a few millimetres and sew a running stitch around the outside, just in from the edge.

3. When you reach the point where you started, continue with another couple of stitches, pull up the thread and flatten the small, puffy bulb you are left with to create a 'flower' shape. Tuck the raw edges inside for a neat finish.

4. Thread needle through the back of the yoyo and sew a few small, firm stitches.

5. When all your yoyos are complete, sew them to the cushion in a cluster, or dotted randomly over its surface or to cover stains. Sew from underneath the yoyo, pulling the front layer of fabric away from the needle so the back is secured but the front stays puffy.

MATERIALS NEEDED FOR A CONTRASTING RUFFLE

- A long strip of cotton, linen or silk – its length will need to be two-and-a-half times the perimeter measurement of your cushion x 12cm (5in), to make a ruffle with a finished width of 5cm (2in)
- Sewing machine and thread
- Needle and thread
- Pins

INSTRUCTIONS FOR RUFFLE

1. Choose fabric for the contrasting ruffle in a shade picked out from one of the existing colours in the cushion's design, or another that completely contrasts; such as green paired with pink or yellow with blue. To save on buying more fabric than you need, stitch strips of fabric together to achieve the desired length (two-and-a-half times the perimeter measurement of your cushion for a really dramatic ruffle, such as this).

2. Fold fabric in half, right sides together, to measure 6cm (2½in) wide. Stitch along raw edges in a straight line to create a tube.

3. Turn right side out by tucking one end inside and shimmying through until the entire tube is turned inside out.

4. Iron flat, pulling out the seams to create an even strip.

5. Insert one end inside the other end of the tube, folding under the raw edges and stitching strip into a large circle.

6. Take needle and double thread (for strength) and tack-stitch (a loose running stitch) along the bottom of the fabric strip, near the seam. When you've tacked all the way along, pull the thread through carefully so it gathers, and work the gathers down along the strip by hand so it's evenly ruffled along the entire circle.

7. Attach ruffle at each corner of the cushion with pins, distributing gathers evenly along each side.

8. Sew to the seams of your cushion by hand or with a sewing machine, with the bottom seam facing to the back of the cushion. To hide the bottom seam of your ruffle completely, you could unpick the seams of your vintage cushion case and poke it inside before sewing it all back together, but this quick-fix works just as well (and can be removed at a later date if you want to change it).

THE CRAFTY MINX *AT HOME*

CONSIDER SPLASHING A CHEEKY MESSAGE ACROSS IT

Buy pearl embroidery thread in a lolly-like selection of colours and chain stitch favourite phrases or words. If you don't feel confident sewing freehand, use a dressmaker's pencil first before picking out in thread. This can be washed or removed with a damp cloth when you're done.

DOLL UP A STUBBORN STAIN

Another tip is to cover stains that just won't budge with a simple silk or embroidery stitch. Draw flowers, hearts, stars or freehand curlicues on with pen, and stitch over with pearl embroidery thread.

Or make your own basic cushion. Read on for instructions on how to do this from scratch with linen and a pretty silk scarf.

MATERIALS NEEDED FOR A SCARF CUSHION

- 53 x 56cm (21 x 22in) cotton, linen or upholstery fabric (for back)
- 53cm (21in) square of silk (for front); an old scarf will do
- Ruler
- Dressmaker's chalk
- Scissors
- 45cm (18in) zipper
- Sewing machine and thread
- Zipper foot
- 50cm (20in) cushion insert

Chain stitch favourite phrases or words

INSTRUCTIONS

1 Measure and cut your fabric rectangle into two pieces: one should be 53 x 14.5cm (21 x 5¾in) and the other should be 53 x 41.5cm (21 x 17in).

2 With right sides together, align the two backing pieces along the 53cm (21in) edge.

3 Take your zip and lay it along this 53cm (21in) edge so that it is equidistant from both ends. Make a mark on the edges of the fabric to show where the zip opening should start and finish.

4 Put the zip aside and, allowing a 1.5cm (½in) seam, sew the seam closed at each end, from your mark to the edge, leaving the seam open in the middle. Press the seam allowance open, pressing open the edges of the unstitched section as well.

5 With the right side of the fabric facing upwards, position your closed zip under the opening (make sure it's facing up the right way) and pin it in place. Pin one folded edge of the opening about 2mm (⅛in) from the zipper teeth and the pin the other side about 1cm (⅜in) from the folded edge. Place a pin across the seam at the top and bottom of the opening, one pin just above the pull tab and the other just below the zip stop. It is a good idea to tack the zip in position now before stitching it, as the pins can get a bit awkward while you stitch.

6 Using a zipper foot on your machine, sew the zip in place, stitching along both sides and pivoting on the needle at the corners to stitch across the top and bottom too.

7 Open the zip slightly. With right sides together, raw edges matching and allowing a 1.5cm (½in) seam, stitch the silk cushion front to the back around all edges.

8 To reduce bulk, carefully cut away the seam allowance to about 5mm (¼in). Snip diagonally across each corner to remove the extra fabric – take care not to cut into your stitching – and turn the cover right side out through the zip opening. Push the corners out with your fingers.

9 Insert the cushion pad into your cover and zip it up.

Tip

If the thought of inserting a zip is putting you off making your own cushion covers, you can make a lapped back opening minus the zip. Alternatively, just leave out the zip and cut the back the same size as the front. Leave one side open for the cushion pad and sew the opening edges of the cover together by hand when you've finished. It surely won't need washing all that often – when it does, simply unpick the seam and sew it up again.

THE CRAFTY MINX *AT HOME*

Absolutely affordable art and old/new framing

My perfect home is quirky, inviting, personal and cosy, and artwork plays a major part in creating this environment. Sheer variety adds texture, and forms an eclectic look overall. There are so many artists whose work I admire but, apart from a few treasured pieces, I haven't bought much art in the past that has any real market value. Cost is prohibitive but it's more about priorities: if you love and appreciate fine art, you'll find money to invest in it.

That said, we've no shortage of treasured pieces competing for prime wall space in our home; everything from photography, textiles and oil paintings to old playbills, lithographs, cute prints, collages, etchings, drawings, ceramics and sculpture. Some I made myself, others were created by my husband or daughter, most were salvaged from flea markets and the rest were found in auction houses or received as gifts.

It's amazing how much fabulous discarded art there is to be found in second-hand stores, flea markets and auction houses. If you couldn't care less about caché and gravitate instead towards pieces that elicit that trusty 'I must have it' reaction, you'll have no trouble finding great pieces to decorate and define your home. Forget about impressing anyone but yourself and your partner. You're the ones who have to live with it, after all.

Following is an inventory of my current favourite vintage and retro pieces. Some are high-quality prints rather than originals, but the framing and mix makes them more unique and unlike anything readily available in stores:

- Original live action photograph from a performance of *Swan Lake* in the 1920s (seen here on the left). I found the picture in a flea market and the frame in a charity store for a few dollars apiece. The mounting and glass are new.
- Original and rare Chinese perfume poster from the 1920s, found in Paris and given a modern frame and mounting treatment (seen resting against the wall on page 182).
- A limited-edition print of the well-known oil painting 'Saw Ohn Nyun' by Sir Gerald Kelly, 1932, in its 1960s-era frame.
- Rare ceramic blue-haired girl, made in 1950s Germany. One day I will find her an appropriate black box frame to live in (see overleaf).
- Two oil paintings, probably from the '50s or '60s, which cost very little from a market and look great, liberated from their original frames and stacked or mounted against the wall.
- A set of '70s-era lithographs from New York, found in a flea market in really damaged, ugly old frames. I had them re-framed with metallic-painted bamboo and pale blush mounting card, with an inner rim of gold and new glass. I call them my Disco Ladies – they look so modern, but I love the fact that they're actually quite old. Even with top-notch framing, they cost significantly less than the sort of mass-manufactured prints found everywhere (one is seen here on the left, the other adorns the bedroom wall on page 127).
- A French pen drawing of a villa called 'Le Mas', date unknown. Found as is for the cost of a few cups of coffee (shown above club lounge on page 57).
- An illustrated, handwritten card for a decadent French meal, dated 29 Avril (April), 1903. Truffles, paté and langoustines were just a few ingredients on the menu (oh, to have been at that table).

MATERIALS FOR TOP-NOTCH OLD AND NEW FRAMING

- Attractive vintage or antique frame, with or without glass
- New glass, cut to size (optional)
- Craft knife
- Cloth and spray cleaner or white vinegar
- Old toothbrush
- Mounting board, purchased from an art supplies store
- Ruler
- Pencil
- Roller cutter and cutting mat
- Illustration, painting or print, either old or new
- Wide masking tape
- Thick card
- Glue
- Small screw-in eye hooks
- Hanging wire
- Pliers

INSTRUCTIONS

1. Use your craft knife to cut away any masking tape, and remove the frame's backing. Pull out the damaged print and cracked or broken glass, wrapping glass carefully in old newspaper before ditching it in the bin.

2. Spray cleaner or white vinegar on frame and wipe away all dust, using an old toothbrush to clean dust from every crevice. Watch out for chipped gilt, and go over carefully with cloth.

3. When your frame is dry, insert new cut-to-size glass (you can order this from a framer's shop when you supply them with measurements) or polish up the original sheet of glass with cleaner and cloth. You might also want to go without – who says all frames need glass covers?

4. Using your ruler and pencil to measure up, cut mounting board to the frame's size with roller cutter on cutting mat, and use ruler to work out the size needed for the middle aperture, where your artwork will be visible. A centre position usually works best (with an equal amount on both sides, and equal amount at top and bottom) but experiment with off-centre mounting if it

takes your fancy. Just remember to allow for 5–10mm ($\frac{1}{4}$–$\frac{3}{8}$ in) overlap on each side so the image edges will be hidden.

5. Following your pencil marks, cut out the aperture in the mounting board with your roller cutter.

6. Taking your thick card and new photograph, print or illustration, glue the back of the image to the card.

7. Insert image in frame and use masking tape to secure in place.

8. Re-install frame backing, using masking tape to secure around all four edges for a professional finish.

9. Screw in your small eye hooks at either side of the frame. You may need to create an initial hole with a hammer and nail before screwing into the wood.

10. Add wire, using pliers to cut off any excess and winding wire around before doubling back for strength. Now you're ready to get hanging.

Top tips for collecting affordable art

❧ Visit exhibitions of new, emerging artists rather than the more established names, and consider buying smaller, unframed pieces. You can always frame them at a later date, or hunt out appropriate second-hand frames in the interim. This allows you to invest in artists you admire without the huge initial outlay. You can also play up the dimensions of a piece with deep-set mounting and an oversized frame.

❧ Find a framer you can trust. The difference between good framing and bad is vast, and if you develop a relationship with someone, chances are they'll offer discounts for repeat business. Don't be afraid to ask 'is that your best price?', because various choices in mounting, frames and glass will make a difference to the final cost, and they can always present you with different options to suit your budget. A decent frame makes the world of difference, and is worth the extra investment.

❧ Ignore ugly frames, discoloured or damaged glass and layers of dust or grime when you love the painting or print itself. These are easily replaced or removed, and your piece will appear far more valuable and stylish once updated.

❧ Buy beautiful frames whenever you see them for a bargain, even when you dislike the work itself. Save for those pieces you do like. New glass comes relatively cheap, and cardboard mounting helps anchor the image to the correct size.

❧ Go for a theme, such as '50s ballerina dancers, floral still-life or landscapes, if you're worried about the flea market effect of too many styles jumbled together, or to unify different pieces. Alternatively, opt for a specific colour palette. Set yourself a budget limit, and enjoy adding to your collection when you come upon pieces that fit within your general theme.

Sew cute
knitting or workbag

Back in the '70s, my grandmother had the funkiest home for the times – all swirly wallpaper and shagpile rugs in various shades of brown, burnt orange and egg yolk. Her console side units alone were enough to make mid-century furniture aficionados go gaga, and a nest of kidney-shaped coffee tables took pride of place in the sitting room. Personally, I adored her set of ladybird fridge magnets, and a faux fur-cushioned powdering chair, which sat near a low dressing table in the corner of her bedroom. Nanna also had plenty of framed tapestries, depicting stallions and saucy blue bare-breasted women, on the walls of her Spanish-style bungalow.

I was very fond of needlepoint kits as a child, but don't actually recall ever finishing one. I imagine it's hugely satisfying, but it's unnecessary to create your own to get a kick out of tapestry. I've been collecting old cross-stitch and needlepoint for aeons, and my favourite way to show it off is by repurposing in quilts or tote bags – still very satisfying as a craft project, but completed in a fraction of the time.

I bought this gorgeous pussycat tapestry for my daughter Olive at a flea market. I love the faded quality of the pink background and the markings on her coat. She's a real charmer, don't you think? One day I might incorporate her into a cushion or blanket, or even a child-sized tote.

I found this French needlepoint in a charity store for only a few dollars. It was mounted in a naff frame and grotty with age, so I used a Stanley knife to liberate the design, gave it a good hand wash and ironed it before creating this handy bag for on-the-go sewing projects.

MATERIALS NEEDED

- Needlepoint, salvaged from an old frame or charity store
- Various fabric scraps
- Contrasting fabrics for back of bag and lining
- 70 x 12cm (27 $\frac{1}{2}$ x 5in) fabric strip, for straps
- Pretty length of vintage edging, rickrack and/or lace
- Scissors
- Sewing machine and thread
- Iron
- Plastic, taken from a cloth supermarket bag or discarded packaging

INSTRUCTIONS

1 Lay needlepoint on table and add pieces of remnant fabric to the sides, top and bottom to create a front panel in your desired size – either a square or a rectangle – allowing for 1cm ($\frac{3}{8}$in) seams on each side. Add vintage rickrack scraps, bias binding or lace for interest, drama, or just to stop it being ordinary. The needlepoint panel in this bag measures 35cm (14in) square, but the bag's finished dimensions are 48cm wide x 35cm high (19 x 14in), once all the pieces are sewn together. You also need to allow about 6cm (2$\frac{1}{2}$in) extra on the bottom edge, because when the lower corners are boxed out, the finished height of your bag will be shorter.

2 To create a more wedge-shaped bag with a wider opening than its base, fold your completed front rectangle in half crosswise and rule a sloping line from the upper corners to a narrower point on the baseline. My bag front is 50cm (20in) across the top edge, tapering to 30cm (12in) across the bottom. Cut along your ruled line and open out again for a wedge-shaped bag front.

3 Now use the front as a pattern to create the back panel and two lining panels, from two pieces of contrasting fabric, such as green-striped mattress ticking, which I used for the lining. You could also cut a pocket-sized rectangle from the lining fabric too, if you like.

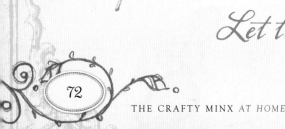

Let the needlepoint or tapestry dictate what you do with it

4 With right sides facing each other and allowing 1cm (³⁄₈in) seams, sew the outer panels of the bag together along the sides and bottom of the bag, leaving the top edge open. Repeat with the lining panels, adding an inside pocket at this stage, if you like. Press all the seams open and leave both bag and lining inside out.

5 To box out the lower corners of the outer bag, creating a flat bottom, fold the lower corner into a triangle, right sides together, so that the side and bottom seams are exactly aligned. From the apex of the triangle, run a ruler down the seam until the base width of the triangle measures 12cm (5in) across – 6cm (2½in) on either side of the seam. Rule a line across the triangle at this point, then stitch along the ruled line. Cut away excess fabric, leaving a 1cm (³⁄₈in) allowance. Repeat this step for the remaining lower corner of the bag, and on both lower corners of the lining too.

6 Fold over 1cm (³⁄₈in) on the top raw edge of the outer bag and iron in place. Repeat with lining.

7 Cut a piece of firm plastic into a 12 x 28cm (5 x 11in) rectangle (or the dimensions of your bag's base) and slip it into the bottom of your outer bag, so that it sits snugly within the seam lines – trim it a little more, if necessary. Now place lining inside outer bag, wrong sides facing each other, and pin upper edges together.

8 For the straps, take a strip of fabric measuring roughly 70 x 12cm (27½ x 5in). Fold in half with right sides together to measure 70 x 6cm (27½ x 2½in), before sewing along the long raw edges. Turn right side out, and press. Cut the strap in half crosswise. If you want to insert plastic carry handles, fold each strap in half lengthwise and topstitch the edges together for about 12cm (5in) in the centre of the strap, creating a flat, open-ended tube. Reinforce the stitching at each end.

9 Pin the raw ends of the straps in place along the upper edge, between the outer bag and lining, about 7cm (3in) in from the sides.

10 Sew the outer bag to the lining in a straight line around the open edges, reversing over the straps for strength and removing pins as you go.

11 For hard carry handles, cut out two strips of plastic, each about 12 x 2cm (5 x ¾in), roll lengthways and insert them into the flat tubes in the handle straps.

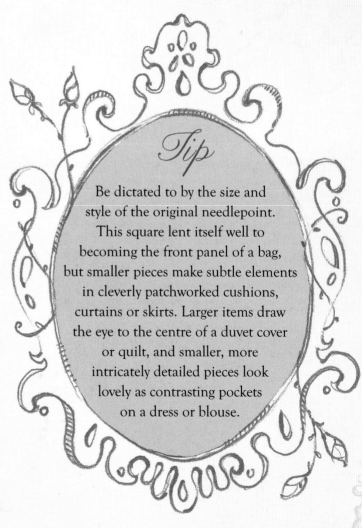

Tip

Be dictated to by the size and style of the original needlepoint. This square lent itself well to becoming the front panel of a bag, but smaller pieces make subtle elements in cleverly patchworked cushions, curtains or skirts. Larger items draw the eye to the centre of a duvet cover or quilt, and smaller, more intricately detailed pieces look lovely as contrasting pockets on a dress or blouse.

Everything in its place
needle and pin case

Having a sewing kit at hand in your sitting room keeps projects close by and ready to work on in stolen moments. It's amazing how much you can achieve in a few short sessions. For me, crochet and sewing are almost meditative – there's nothing quite like the state I can lull myself into by being creative. The closest feeling otherwise is achieved during yoga or actual meditation.

Now you have a nifty sewing bag to store half-done projects, you'll need somewhere to keep all your sharp bits and bobs without fear of injury. No blood on the projects, please (or sweat and tears, come to think of it). This needle case is so simple to make but effectively holds all your pins and needles in place, stops nasty accidents while fossicking around in your cavernous work kit, and looks super kawaii to boot.

MATERIALS NEEDED

- Lovely wool felt – I've used tan, red and cream Heather Bailey designer felt
- Scissors
- Pinking shears
- Red and white pearl embroidery thread
- Needle
- Small button
- Needle and pin collection (to use and store in finished case)

PATTERN

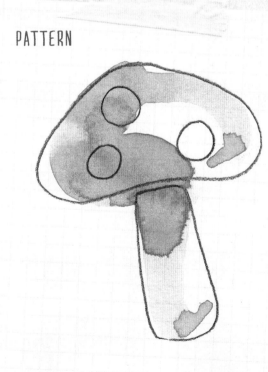

Keep projects close by to work on in stolen moments

INSTRUCTIONS

1 Cut out a rectangle of tan felt measuring 22 x 14cm (9 x 5½in), and a smaller strip, measuring 7 x 2cm (3 x ¾in), for the closing strap.

2 Use pinking shears to cut out a smaller rectangle of cream felt, measuring 20 x 12cm (8 x 5in).

3 Cut out toadstool shapes from red and cream felt, using the pattern shown on page 75.

4 Place cream felt rectangle on top of tan rectangle, equidistant from each edge. Sew with machine or by hand in a straight line down the centre of both.

5 Place the smaller strip in the middle of the back 'page' of tan felt, and sew into place.

6 Fold over to the front, work out where the button should be to secure strap in place, and sew on.

7 Cut a small hole in the felt strap until the button fits through snugly. Place toadstool shapes on front of the tan felt cover and sew in place with pearl embroidery thread.

8 Use white pearl thread and a chain stitch to cover stitching at the side binding, and you're done.

Tip

Add small straps to the pages of your needle case to store all manner of useful bits and bobs, depending on the items you use most. Think scissors, Quick Unpicks and a selection of various needles.

This is the life
lap blanket

Never throw out your old jumpers when they become pilled, shrunken or holey, and particularly cherish any outgrown pieces that were once loved and well-worn by your children. Re-use them in a wide variety of ways by creating throws, cushions, scarves, hot water bottle covers and soft toys for a newborn, chopping around any stains or holes and creating sturdy seams by hand or with your sewing machine. Incorporate them into new craft projects to extend their usefulness for years to come, and provide loved ones with a wonderful reminder of their childhood or the times they were worn before being re-imagined.

The useful item on the right has led a number of lives. Starting out with a pile of 100% cashmere and lambswool jumper scraps collected from charity stores and flea markets, I initially chopped up the squares to create a woolly winter poncho. The poncho then transformed into a big, cosy wrap when I grew bored and unpicked it, before being unpicked again and repurposed as a blanket for my sickly two-year-old. That's when I added the Liberty print bias binding to its edges.

My recycled jumpers now find most use as a lap blanket in winter while I'm craft-making on the sofa. A bit nanna, I know, but so warm and cosy on the pins and wonderfully warm for a child to curl up in.

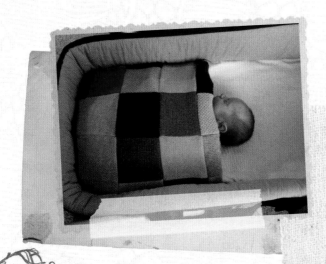

This is my friends Lisa and Trevor's newborn, Thomas, snuggled up in a cot-sized blanket I made from small squares, on his first day home from hospital. Apart from sleep (or a big box of fresh food), I can't think of a better gift for first-time parents.

MATERIALS NEEDED

- A selection of lovely old holey or stained jumpers, ripe for chopping up
- Ruler
- Scissors
- Sewing machine or needle and thread
- Rotary cutter, mat and quilting rule (optional)
- Bias binding, enough to cover all four edges

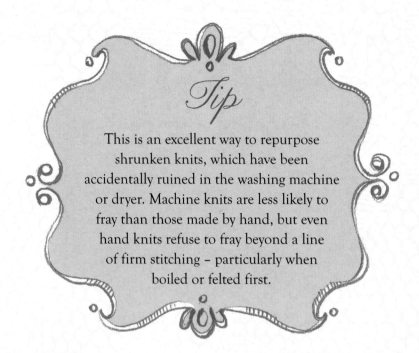

Tip

This is an excellent way to repurpose shrunken knits, which have been accidentally ruined in the washing machine or dryer. Machine knits are less likely to fray than those made by hand, but even hand knits refuse to fray beyond a line of firm stitching – particularly when boiled or felted first.

INSTRUCTIONS

1 Collect old jumpers in roughly the same weight and stitch size, and in a variety of colours. Mine were literally scraps before I started, left over from other craft projects such as hot water bottle covers and scarves.

2 Cut around damaged areas and seams to create 72 squares, measuring 12 x 12cm (5 x 5in) each. (This will make a small lap rug or cot blanket; you will need at least 90 squares for a larger rug.)

3 Lay squares on table or floor and shuffle them about until you're happy with the overall effect, for a finished rectangle of eight squares wide x nine squares long (or larger, if using more squares). A random layout looks most charming.

4 Start sewing together one line at a time, with a small stitch on the sewing machine, or by hand.

5 When you're done, use a quilting rule and rotary cutter to even up the edges or trim carefully by hand.

6 Find cotton or silk bias binding in a complementary fabric to cover all four edges (make sure to buy a little more than you think you need, as it's very frustrating to run out). Sew binding around the blanket on the wrong side, before folding over edge and stitching flat. Or buy 25mm- (1in-) wide binding and simply fold it over the edge of the blanket, before sewing both sides together on the machine, with the blanket secured between them.

ALL FUN AND PARLOUR GAMES

The Loo table (a small table with shaped top that can be tilted and pushed into a corner) was a piece of furniture, created during the Victorian era, that evolved with the popularity of parlour games. Particularly favoured by ladies of means looking to fill their days, the name comes from a much-played card game of the time, 'Loo'.

There is a popular misconception surrounding the name of these tables. Many think they were designed for occasional use in the toilet or have something to do with Napoleon – both incorrect.

Thinking space

THE CREATIVE STUDY
OR WRITING DESK

Ever since I started working from home, I've relished the freedom of being able to open my laptop and create a study area wherever I happen to be – whether that's propped up in bed, reclining on the sofa, out in the garden or (most likely) perched at the kitchen table next to a steaming pot of tea.

We have a spare room, but it's darker than our sun-filled kitchen and far less spacious, so it tends to make me feel hemmed-in or back in the grey-walled work cubicle of my old office environment. I also miss the bustle of family life, preferring the background noise of the radio, my three-year-old tearing about and husband banging about with pots and pans over silence, while attending to light tasks such as email. For serious writing and contemplation, I wait until I'm alone and settle down to work at the kitchen table, teacup and a snacking bowl of granola within close reach.

Adopt an air of industry and
the real deal will follow

But just because I don't have an official workspace, doesn't mean I don't long to, some day. My dream study involves a simple chair, a wooden desk topped with a potted orchid or vase of pink peonies, and my laptop. Nothing else, bar perhaps a notepad and fountain pen.

And an open window to gaze out across the rooftops from. A harbour view or ocean vista really would take the cake, but a roof and treetops scene would also suit me just fine. I know it'll happen eventually, and in the interim, I'm already there in my head.

An uncluttered desk = a focused mind. Create space to think clearly and be productive, and let the perfect study of your imagination sustain you: you'll be amazed at what it's possible to accomplish, when you adopt an air of industry.

THE EVOLUTION OF THE DESK

THE CRAFTY MINX *AT HOME*

If we spend a third of our lives in bed then surely most of us spend at least another third in front of our desks.

The desk comes in many guises – from a plain rectangle with no ornamentation to a wonderful extension of the self. Another creation that started out life as something else and grew legs, the humble desk was originally a simple slab of wood placed atop a pedestal, which grew in stature and popularity as people learned to read and write.

Given that so few people had mastered written communication before this time, apart from an elite few, it's no surprise that desks have played a vital role in our history, as the site where treaties between countries have been signed, constitutions formed, and the great letters and writing of our past created. This is why certain desks are now housed in museums, and the desk came to be considered such a status symbol.

With the constant movement of the landed gentry, the pedestal desk first found favour. Consisting of three pieces (a top on two pedestals), it was perfect for use when the court was on tour between stately homes. Many desks made in the 19th century were constructed with three pieces for ease of transportation, and 'Campaign' furniture also included desks that could be taken out into the field and unhinged in moments, easily recognised by their sectional appearance and dark mahogany, with shiny brass hinges and carrying handles.

A fine example of an early desk is Henry VIII's writing desk. Dated 1525, it is made from walnut and oak and lined with leather. Also painted and gilded with the king's coat of arms, Henry's was more of a portable lap desk for getting about (he being busy with the English Reformation, multiple marriages and so forth).

As with most pieces of furniture, fashions started at the top with those in the court, and flowed down the social ladder to the general public. Jacob Frères, furniture makers to Louis XIV, were the leaders in fashion and their Bureau du Roi (housed in the Wallace collection in London) is indeed something to behold. Regency dandies favoured expensive Boulle work and brass and tortoiseshell inlays, and desks became known for the shapes given to them by either the stately home that they were designed for or their wealthy patron (or, at very least, their designer).

Names such as the 'Carlton House' (noted for its useful galleried top and curved back), the 'Davenport' (a small, portable sloping pedestal containing drawers), and the 'Cutler' roll top desk (which is of unproven origin but has many claims to fame) were most popular. The Cutler is still produced today and, in its heyday in mid-Victorian times, was considered a wonderful way to have a messy desk – complete with quill feathers and half-written love letters – which could be easily concealed and locked with the roll of a tambour shutter. Its popularity declined with the advent of the computer, as the CRT screens were too big to fit under the roll, but now computers have slimmed down, its fortunes may turn once again.

Simply swellegant
handmade cards

Inside my capacious crafts cabinet is a vintage biscuit tin filled to the brim with tiny fabric scraps, leftover from various sewing projects. Even those measuring a few centimetres or less find themselves saved from the bin and used for homemade cards, invitations and thank you messages. Larger fragments are turned into yoyos, bows and abstract forms to adorn high-quality parchment, often layered over delicate rice and origami paper, and all stitched together by hand or machine. Well-thumbed magazines also find themselves repurposed in this way. Topped off with a cute antique button or ribbon scrap, such creations can amount to miniature works of art.

On wet weekends, I love nothing more than spending a few hours lost in the escapism of card making. Prepare a stack for the stationery drawer, to hand over to friends with birthday gifts, as thank you notes, for invitations and just-because occasions, and experience a sense of delayed gratitude when you find them available at a moment's notice, avoiding a trip to the shops.

THE CRAFTY MINX AT HOME

I regret not buying a box full of vintage
stamps I once spied at an auction
house – it included over 200 in various
motifs such as 1920s-era flappers, cars,
puppies and aeroplanes. I've seen lesser
collections sold at astronomical prices
ever since. Snap up vintage stamps if
you're fortunate enough to find them –
they certainly pay for themselves
over time through constant re-use.

THE CRAFTY MINX AT HOME

MATERIALS NEEDED

- Fabric and paper scraps – small, spriggy florals, such as any leftover Tana Lawn Liberty print fabric, or Japanese origami paper look particularly fetching

- A5 parchment or thin cardboard

- Scissors

- Tacky craft glue

- Needle or sewing machine and thread – opt for lovely metallics if you can

INSTRUCTIONS

1. Make cards that are quirky, cute and personal by playing around with fabric on paper for abstract designs, or cut out basic shapes appropriate for all sorts of occasions, such as stars, hearts and birds.

2. Fix in place with a dab of glue.

3. Sew together on the machine or by hand.

4. Buy envelopes to fit, or make your own to match with parchment, by folding over and sewing up the sides.

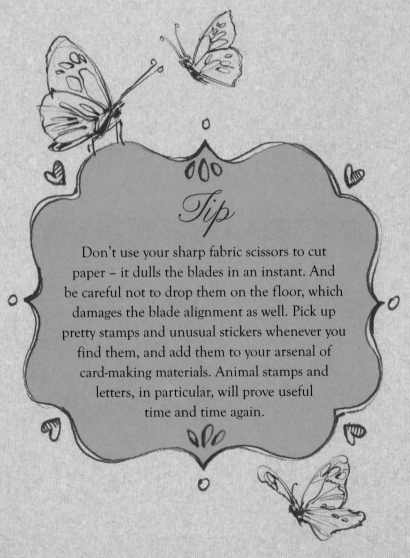

Tip

Don't use your sharp fabric scissors to cut paper – it dulls the blades in an instant. And be careful not to drop them on the floor, which damages the blade alignment as well. Pick up pretty stamps and unusual stickers whenever you find them, and add them to your arsenal of card-making materials. Animal stamps and letters, in particular, will prove useful time and time again.

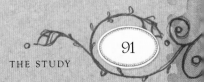

Cheer up a dull work area with
fancy oddments and vintage treasures

Out-there
in-tray

Personalise your workspace with a versatile cloth in-tray. Easily crafted from upholstery fabric remnants or heavyweight canvas, it'll cheer up any dull work area.

These A4-sized trays work a treat for storing bills and any loose papers, and aren't so deep that you tend to lose important papers under a mountain of forgotten correspondence.

MATERIALS NEEDED

- Three different upholstery fabric remnants, canvas or similar heavyweight fabrics
- Ruler
- Dressmaker's chalk
- Dressmaker's scissors
- Sewing machine and thread

INSTRUCTIONS

1 The finished size of this tray is 33cm (13in) long by 24cm (9½in) wide by 8cm (3¼in) high. From Fabric 1, cut two rectangles, each 35 x 18cm (14 x 17in), for the long sides; from Fabric 2, cut two rectangles, each 26 x 18cm, (10¼ x 7in) for the shorter sides; from Fabric 3, cut two rectangles, 35 x 26cm (14 x 10¼in), for the inside and base.

2 With right sides together and allowing 1cm (³⁄₈in) seams, join the two shorter side rectangles to each side of the base, along the 26cm (10¼in) edges.

3 Add the inside rectangle along the 26cm (10¼in) edge of one short side as well – you should now have a long strip of fabric, consisting of four rectangles.

4 Add the longer side rectangles to each side of the base. Now sew up the remaining edges, one after another, right sides together, to form a three-dimensional inside-out box shape.

5 Leave the inside shorter edge open, but sew ends together by a few centimetres (an inch).

6 Turn right side out through the opening and pop corners into place, with the base folding down to sit beneath. Use your fingers to fold and smooth the sides into position.

7 Lastly, fold under the remaining raw edges and use your machine to sew the opening closed.

Film noir furniture

I've always fancied the sort of study seen in old '40s films – something like the office in the classic Humphrey Bogart film *The Maltese Falcon*, with a wooden filing cabinet, desk, angle-poise lamp and chair designed well before we started worrying about ergonomics. As a fan of '40s fashion, I imagine the furnishings paired with a bold-shouldered blazer from the era, similar to those worn by Bogey's co-star, Mary Astor. What a killer look. It's a shame the typewriter is dead – this dated study accoutrement looks great, even just for show. Hunt down new typewriter ribbon, and tap away at greeting cards or place settings for typography with nostalgia. (I won't be tapping out my next book with this old Royal-brand typewriter though – that is certain.)

Head to auction houses and flea markets for the best bargains on study-appropriate furniture, and soften up the schoolhouse strictness of darker woods with quirky ceramics and textiles, or reinvent with a bold coat of paint.

My old work desk looks atmospheric topped with all my vintage oddments and ceramics, and glass receptacles storing paperclips, pens and other useful items, and the banker's lamp is from the UK, via a local auction house. In any study used mainly for show, you can't go past an old Bakelite telephone. Bring antique phones out of retirement with a modern adaptor, and enjoy the true vintage *brrrring* when someone calls.

Beaux-arts bookends

I'm not a huge fan of dust-collecting bits and bobs or anything remotely capable of carrying the title of 'knick-knacks', but I do love a few special display pieces made from ceramic or bone china, arranged on a sparsely decorated shelf. Think Japanese-style Art of Placement, with beautiful handmade bowls and plates, because they're utilitarian as well as beautiful and cleverly store found objects, such as shells, sea glass, and other random items. Carefully selected figurines also make a rare appearance, and add their own quirky charm to any decorative set-up.

Ceramic figurines can be found in the most ordinary of charity stores and indeed any second-hand marketplace, and retail for anything from 50 cents to hundreds of dollars – a far cry from the thousands fetched at auction houses for coveted items such as flapper figurines from the art deco period. But my advice is to ignore the origin, and opt instead for pieces that appeal to you. This could be anything from Bambi-like deer figurines to dancing ladies or a strutting horse – whatever floats your boat.

Consider unusual displays, or turn figurines into a set of bookends; these can be a gorgeous thing to show off on a desk or mantelpiece, along with a few favourite books. The idea behind these is to modernise the dated figurine by turning it into something new and covetable once again. And with a few pieces of wonderfully aged or reclaimed wood to add them to, you might even have a family heirloom in the making.

MATERIALS NEEDED

- Reclaimed wood or MDF
- Saw
- Hammer and nails and/or glue
- Paint and paintbrush (optional)
- Two ceramic figurines
- Two metal brackets, available from a hardware store

THE CRAFTY MINX AT HOME

INSTRUCTIONS

1 Take your pieces of MDF or reclaimed wood and fit together to form an L-shape, taking the height and width of a standard hardcover novel as your cue to size.

2 Nail both pieces together and/or apply wood glue to secure in place. If your wood and glue job looks a bit iffy, paint over the incriminating evidence in a shade that flatters the chosen figurine or makes it stand out, such as black or white.

3 Add metal bracket with glue. It should sit at the base, so the entire construction looks like an upside down 'T'.

4 Decide whether the ceramic figurine looks better facing to the left or right, and glue into place in the centre of the L's base. Again, if the paint on your figurine has rubbed away or looks tired (despite a fetching shape), paint over the ceramic as well with a specialist ceramic paint – one uniform shade looks coolly chic.

5 Repeat with the opposing bookend.

A VERY LITERARY ACCOUTREMENT

Bookends were first used in Victorian times and started out as 'book slides' – a sort of hinged tray-with-sides affair that opened up to hold a small quantity of books. The idea was for a Gent to carry his books from library to study, keeping them orderly whilst off the shelves and returning them whenever his necessary research was concluded.

Typical slides from the Victorian era were made from mahogany with an intricate inlay of mother-of pearl, ivory, cabochon and semi-precious stones, as well as brass hinges and bindings. This nifty device later developed into the bookends we are familiar with today, in all their various guises. From plain L-shapes to galloping horses, finial-style baubles and industrial letters, this relatively new creation is generally used for show, but a fine set makes a handsome addition to any modern household.

THE CRAFTY MINX *AT HOME*

She's got personality
pin board

I've always found mood boards intriguing – take a peek inside any designer or artist's studio, and you will usually find their inspirations tacked up on pin boards or the walls, showing the influences for any given season or collection. It can be a real insight into what makes them tick.

My own cork-based mood board is pinned with a variety of objects, both found and gifted; pretty fabric and paint swatches, favourite thank you cards and postcards from friends, my daughter's childish, colourful scribblings, the details of useful businesses and suppliers, feathers and jewellery and inspiring postcard-sized artwork prints by the likes of Gustav Klimt and Lucien Freud.

Padded pin boards provide a lovely way to decorate the study while being equally useful for display. Offering a space for temporarily displaying cards, ticket stubs, photographs and illustrations, they're also perfect for storing reminders and bills to be paid, and keeping important tasks front of mind.

MATERIALS NEEDED

- Plain corkboard – these are inexpensive and easy to find at hardware or homewares stores
- A layer of medium-thickness batting (enough to cover the size of your pin board – polyester is fine)
- Dressmaker's scissors
- Craft glue
- Fabric to cover pin board, with a few centimetres (an inch) to spare around all four edges
- Staple gun and staples
- Ribbon
- Ruler
- Pin tacks

INSTRUCTIONS

1   Place your corkboard on a flat surface, right side up, and use as a template for cutting out the batting to fit over its front. Your batting should sit flush with the edges of the board or just inside the edge of the board's frame.

2   Use glue to stick the batting to the cork's surface.

3   Lay out your fabric, right side down, and centre the board on it, batting side down.

4   Cut around the outside of the board's frame, leaving a few centimetres (an inch) of fabric spare along each side.

5   Mitre the edges by folding each corner down first and stapling it into place, making sure the fabric at the front is taut and even across the front surface. Then, neatly fold in the excess fabric on each edge of the corner so that the folded edges meet at the centre, and staple in place. Turn under the raw edges of the remaining fabric by a few millimetres (1/4 in), and staple the folded edge to the back of the frame, close to the fabric's edge.

6   Continue turning under and stapling fabric to the back of the frame, placing a staple every 2.5cm (1in) or so around the perimeter of the frame.

7   Take the ribbon, and staple one end to a corner at the back of the frame, right side facing up. Fold the ribbon over the front surface of the board and loop over diagonally opposite corner before cutting off ribbon and stapling this end into place.

8   Repeat for the other diagonal corners, so the ribbon is crossed at the front of the board.

9   Now measure 15cm (6in) from one line of ribbon, and place further lengths of ribbon at intervals along the board, stapling them into place to create diamond shapes. Continue until done.

10   Use the pin tacks to secure the ribbons where they intersect. You are now ready to mount your pin board and start creating your very own mood display.

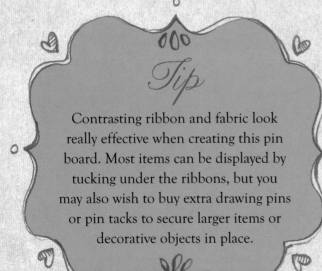

Tip

Contrasting ribbon and fabric look really effective when creating this pin board. Most items can be displayed by tucking under the ribbons, but you may also wish to buy extra drawing pins or pin tacks to secure larger items or decorative objects in place.

Dreamtime

SHRINE-TO-SLEEP BEDROOMS

The vast majority of us live in cities, and inner-city living tends to equal small living spaces and even smaller bedrooms. If you can create a peaceful sanctuary in the bedroom, free from clutter, I'm convinced it makes for a better night's sleep, daytime escape vault and calmer mind in general.

A decade ago, I lived in high-charged Hong Kong, where apartment sizes are calculated in square feet to include not only your home, but all the shared spaces within a multi-story building complex. Five hundred square feet is considered generous, and 1,000+ positively luxurious. In these sort of environs, clever layout and storage solutions are essential. I try recalling my zen, feng shui'd Hong Kong apartment – filled with very few belongings at the time, because I didn't own many – whenever I'm considering the purchase of anything, and look to a couple I know who live in a Sydney studio apartment near Centennial Park (with a dog: a Labrador, no less) for inspiration: buy only what you love or will use. Everything else is junk. The lesson was driven home recently when putting half our house in storage for a possible move: we need so little to live comfortably, really.

Make it serene

BEDROOM ESSENTIALS ARE THUS:

- A bed to lay your head upon, of course, fitted with the best mattress and highest thread count Egyptian cotton bed linen you can afford
- Bedside tables, drawers or boxes to store glasses, books and other bedtime necessities
- A lamp or two for late-night reading
- Art, hung above the bed or directly opposite (to appease the soul)
- In the absence of fitted carpet, a rug or comforting sheepskin to cover bare boards
- A chair for taking shoes on or off and draping discarded clothes over when in a rush
- If you don't have the luxury of a separate dressing room or walk-in robe, an excellent wardrobe with well laid out internal storage

That's it. Forget the overflowing bookcases, chi-churning mirrors and whatnots, and the detritus of a busy family life. Anything you haven't read/worn/used in the past two years should be moved on, if not to a friend or charity store then to another part of the house, and the World's Best Mum plaque from your seven-year-old relegated to the fridge or kitchen, where visual clutter can be charming. Responsibilities require downtime, and often the only place to accommodate this is in the bedroom.

If refreshing sleep is necessary for a sane and productive life, consider this: shouldn't we do everything within our power to fulfil this most basic of needs?

Just the two of us
screen-printed pillowcases and cushions

It may be messy business, but screen-printing is not so difficult to master and can be extremely satisfying to complete at home once you've pulled together a basic kit. If you really fall in love with the craft, one day you might consider using more technical methods, such as photo emulsion stencil-making and purchasing your own fancy heat-setter, but overleaf is everything you'll need to start experimenting creatively.

Silk screen-printing can be used on chintzy or striped tea towels, art paper, vintage fabric squares mounted for a wall hanging and, of course, T-shirts and clothing. Plain pillowcases and cushions also provide a perfectly sized canvas to play with, and make wonderful gifts for friends. Fashion a set for your own bed or present to favourite people on the occasion of their wedding.

The fish pattern I've used here was easily created by drawing freehand onto a piece of A4 computer paper, then cut out and screen-printed for my own unique design. Look to abstract shapes or favourite motifs for inspiration – even the simplest can be really effective (crowns, fleurs-de-lys, birds or simply triangles, for example) or blow up my pattern here.

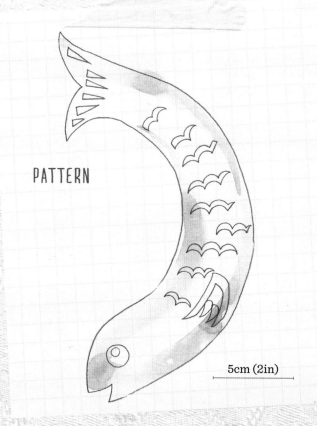

PATTERN

5cm (2in)

Cushions and pillowcases provide a perfect canvas to experiment upon

MATERIALS NEEDED

- A few sheets of A4 or A3 computer paper (depending on the size of your screen)
- Pencil
- Craft knife
- Masking tape
- Silk screen, available from an art supplies store (a long-term investment, which is costly if you're only planning on using it the once but will last a long time for more printing in future). You could also consider making your own
- Squeegee
- Water-based and washable screen-printing fabric ink
- Hair dryer

Tip

Do a test first on disposable fabric before you print your first pillowcase or cushion cover – this way you can see if it's going to turn out the way you envisioned, or whether further experimentation is needed to get the stencil right. Also consider adding lovely embroidery, beading or other decoration to your stencilled designs for a layered and textured finished item.

INSTRUCTIONS

1. Draw or trace your pattern or image onto paper. The larger the form, the easier it will be to perform the next few steps, so perhaps start out with a fairly basic pattern and plan to graduate to more complex shapes later on.

2. When you've finished drawing, use your knife to cut out the design – you want the stencil bit, not the smaller bits (discard these).

3. Tape off the edges on the underside of your screen where the screen will be touching the fabric – you don't want ink leaking around the edges – and place the stencil on top (don't tape your stencil to the mesh, though). Be conscious that you're going to end up with colour in the spaces, and no paint where the paper sits.

4. Lay your test fabric or cushion flat, and place the screen with its stencil over the centre.

5. Apply a good dollop of ink along the top edge of the screen, hold onto the screen firmly, and use your squeegee to scrape down slowly and firmly over the stencil at a 45-degree angle. You'll notice the stencil's now stuck to the screen with ink.

6. Repeat the last step, and place squeegee aside.

7. If you want to make any further prints, make them now and do it quickly – once the ink dries, it will be difficult to remove from the screen.

8. Peel off your stencil, wash the screen carefully with a dish brush or sponge, and set out to dry.

9. Use your hair dryer on the hottest setting to help the drying process and set the paint.

10. Start decorating with beaded additions, embroidery and bias binding, as I've done here. So romantic, *non*?

THE CRAFTY MINX AT HOME

Layer cake
bedside lamp

Lamps make a fine addition to any room, casting soft light and adding quirky charm if chosen for an unusual base or shade. Similar to cushions, a unique table or floor lamp can really change the mood and look of a space and is relatively easy to re-work or swap when seeking a new look, by playing around with different combinations of base and shade.

Browsing through homewares stores, there's often a broad array to choose from, but when settling upon one you love it's almost guaranteed you'll spot it in someone else's place soon after (at least, that's been my experience). The key is to pair vintage bases with new shades for a combination that no-one else has. Or customise an old shade and match it with a sleek new base – this looks fresh, fun and fiercely individual.

MATERIALS NEEDED

- Plain lampshade
- Scraps of linen, hemp or other heavyweight fabric
- Bias binding, to cover top edge of lampshade
- Iron
- Dressmaker's scissors
- Glue gun
- Tacky craft glue

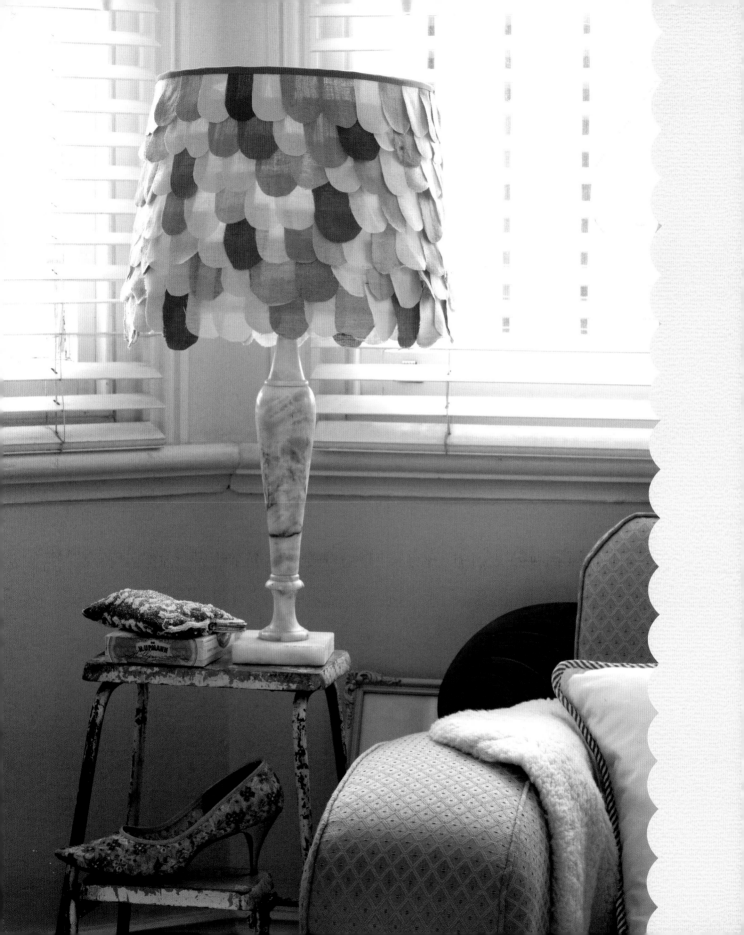

INSTRUCTIONS

1. Settle upon one or a selection of colours, and work out which tone you'd like to have dominate in your lampshade. I've chosen off-white with earthy tones of orange, red, green and a dash of yellow.

2. Iron your linen scraps flat and start cutting in the rough shape of leaves or tongues, as seen here. By cutting freehand rather than to a uniform pattern, the sizes will vary but look more unique when layered upon each other.

3. When you've chopped up a good number of linen pieces (the number depends upon the size of your lampshade and frequency of layers) heat up your glue gun.

4. Apply a small blob of glue to the back of a linen shape, and stick to the bottom of the shade so it hangs over the lower edge.

5. Keep adding until you've reached the end of the row, tucking the last piece under the first.

6. Repeat with each layer until you reach the top of the shade.

7. When all the linen shapes have been applied, lay out bias binding on a table and dab small spots of tacky craft glue along its length.

8. Fold binding over the top edge of the shade, working your way around until the entire length has been secured. Tuck the raw edge of the binding under itself and add a final dab of glue to finish.

Tip

Collect offcuts and remainder pieces of heavy linen and dye to achieve custom colours that complement your bedding or room. Mix up a colour especially, or simply add the random pieces to the pot when you're dyeing clothes or larger pieces of fabric before chopping to size.

Strive for fresh, fun and fiercely original lamps

Dream a little dream
bedside tables

A bedside drawer and the objects it contains provide an interesting insight into a person's character, reminding me of the Natalie Merchant song, 'Jealousy', where she keens about the novels by her lover's bed. Indeed, I enjoy peeking at the novels by a person's bed when I have the opportunity, although I hope I'd never be tempted to open a drawer. My own bedside table is quite personal, not least because it contains the notebook I have on hand for half-asleep midnight scribblings. My insomnia-addled brain is a place I'd rather not share with anyone.

Often a room is completely transformed with one bold or well-judged item of decor. Complement plain, soothing tones in the bedroom with a decorative statement, such as covering your bedside tables with faded vintage wallpaper. This looks unusual and charming, without screaming antique excess.

I've been collecting vintage wallpaper for a while now without a specific purpose in mind, but always seem to find some use for it. Wallpaper makes a great material to decoupage larger pieces of furniture with, and also works well for small alcoves and feature walls. Brilliant when applied to the back wall of a display case or kitchen hutch, it's great as well for covering books and photo albums.

THE CRAFTY MINX AT HOME

Transform a room with homespun decorative statements

MATERIALS NEEDED

- Bedside tables – old ones with a scratched or damaged veneer will do. An auction house is your best bet for a bargain set
- Length of vintage wallpaper
- Sandpaper and block
- Cloth
- Ruler and set square
- Craft knife
- Decoupage glue (or PVA glue mixed 3:1 with water)
- Clear lacquer or varnish
- Paintbrush

INSTRUCTIONS

1 Sand back the wooden surface on your table, and remove all dust with a damp cloth until completely smooth.

2 Measure all of your bedside table's surfaces, including the front of each drawer box if you'd like to cover these, and cut precise shapes from your wallpaper length using the ruler and set square and your craft knife.

3 Apply glue to the furniture surface (rather than the paper) and glue pieces into place. You should use enough glue to make a good bond, but not too much. Smooth surfaces down flat using the ruler, to avoid glue and air bubbles forming between furniture surface and the paper. Wipe over with a damp cloth to remove any excess glue that has squeezed out at the edges. Allow the glue to dry completely.

4 Once the glue is dry, carefully paint over the entire piece of furniture with six to eight coats of clear lacquer, allowing each coat to dry completely before applying the next.

THE CRAFTY MINX AT HOME

Tip

Avoid obvious brush strokes and eradicate
any thicker blobs of varnish with a damp
cloth or by using small, even brush
strokes. This gives your table an even
surface, and ensures you won't end up
with a horrible, stuck-on effect.

MORE THAN SLEEPING QUARTERS

THE NOT-SO-PRIVATE LIFE OF BEDS

Previously functional and undecorated objects, with no-nonsense mortice and tenon joinery, rope cradles and straw mattresses, beds became rather extravagant affairs around about the 17th century, morphing into elegant fashion statements – particularly in the palaces of Europe, where it was the norm to be featured in matters of state. Believe it or not, the ruling monarchy once conducted state business from the comfort of their mattresses. Beds were also used for receptions on the occasion of a birth, death or marriage and, as a rule of thumb, the more social the bed owner, the more decorative it was. Bigger certainly equalled better.

A wonderful example of a Renaissance piece still in existence today is the Great Bed of Ware. Dated circa 1600, this is a carved four-poster bed with a headboard of inlaid marquetry, which is remarkable for its size (326cm wide, or 10ft 9in) and currently exhibited in London's Victoria & Albert Museum. The patterns derive from wood inlaid into wood and show carved figures, which would have once been painted brightly. It could sleep up to 15 people, and was most likely created as an attraction for an inn in Ware, Hertfordshire (and for other reasons I'll leave up to your imagination). Visitors would carve their initials or apply red wax seals after their stays, some of which are still visible on the bedposts and headboard today. The Great Bed of Ware may well be the most famous bed in history, as it was mentioned in Shakespeare's play *Twelfth Night*.

Saucy fact: we often think the waterbed was invented by the baby boomers in that most illustrious of decades, the 1960s. But while the invention of technologically advanced, man-made materials certainly helped propel waterbeds into everyday existence, the ancient Persians also filled goat skins with water well over 3000 years ago for exactly the same reasons ... the details of which escape my delicate sensibilities, but are titillating to say the least. Who knew?

THE CRAFTY MINX AT HOME

A fine marriage
vintage quilts

It's difficult to place value on a beautifully handmade quilt constructed for the home or loved ones. I never imagined I would make my own intricately patchworked quilt. If you'd asked a few years ago I'd have said, *too hard.* Then, I preferred simple squares worked together to create a harmonious palette and, if I'm honest, thought traditional quilts were dated. What a dill. Anyone worth their salt knows the value of a lovingly handmade quilt, constructed patiently over time and displayed upon the bed or a wall. Not least because it contains the memories of cleverly patchworked pieces that retain some essence of their former life. Read *How to Make an American Quilt* by Whitney Otto or watch the film starring Winona Ryder for inspiration, and you'll understand what I mean. The very best kind of quilts are made from a treasure trove of memories in fabric: a favourite dress or print, clothes your children have grown out of, a vintage tablecloth and an eclectic mix of old and new.

The reason for my own quilt volte-face is this: the new guard. There's a whole new industry out there creating fresh fabrics, quilting designs, and simply knockout materials, ripe for discovery by all intrepid crafters. And the best thing is, they're absolutely gorgeous paired with quality vintage pieces. It's a fine marriage indeed. We've come quite a long way since the '70s, the last time crafts were truly trendy. The new guard has brought fresh blood into this once-stagnant industry, and there is much to covet amongst its divine new wares. Paired with modern upcycling, quilting is an incredibly ethical way to re-use stained or holey vintage fabrics, by chopping around areas of damage to salvage the bits worth saving. My fabric obsession is on a par with my fashion lust these days (yet another thing I never thought I'd say).

Specifically, it was a fascination with delicately printed fabrics and silky embroidery thread that first drew me in to quilting. And bias binding to contrast, which I've become nigh on obsessed with. I realised I had everything needed to construct not one, but a whole selection of quilts, just sitting in my crafts cupboard already, before even starting. But where to begin?

I have no patience for tricky quilt patterns and the more painstakingly slow, traditional processes. After signing up to a beginners' class in string-piecing at my favourite haberdashery, Calico & Ivy, I found the permission I needed to break the rules. It was love at first stitch. Instructed by irreverent quilting veteran Sheena ('if it doesn't fit, just chop it off') the craft suddenly seemed much more fun. I'm a convert, can't you see?

For speedy results, try the cheat's method: string-piecing, a clever patchworking technique which will see you completing a full quilt top within a couple of days.

String-piecing is all about breaking the rules to create a complex-looking quilt top in a fraction of the time, by sewing thin strips of fabric together and playing with layout to gorgeous effect. Areas of string-piecing are built upon with freestyle patchworking to follow a general theme of 'whatever looks best', and later quilted together by hand-stitching for a charmingly handmade finish.

Some will tell you you're not really quilting if you're not following a geometric pattern or sticking to the craft's conventions. Just smile sweetly and forge your own path – that's the way of the truly creative.

This is quilting for lazy girls.

*Quilts contain a treasure
trove of memories in fabric*

Sheena says you should always
name your quilts. This is 'Christmas
at Kew Gardens', named after the red,
white and green colour palette and the
place my husband and I used to visit
often when we lived in London.

MATERIALS NEEDED

- Clothing scraps, a vintage tablecloth or tea towels featuring chintzy florals and small lengths of complementary fabric, both old and new – including cross-stitched handkerchiefs and neutral-toned linens. Quantities are not included here because it really depends on the size of your finished quilt (aim for a finished size of about 1.5m (1½yd) square to start with, which is easily manageable). Plan to patchwork pieces together until you're satisfied with the result, before buying backing fabric, batting and bias binding to fit

- Bed sheet or length of contrasting fabric, for backing

- Sheet of very thin batting such as Quilt-Light (perfect for hand-quilting, as not too thick)

- Rotary cutter, cutting mat and quilting rule

- Sewing machine and thread

- Iron

- Scissors

- Safety pins

- 25mm- (1in-) wide bias binding

- Pearl embroidery thread

- Embroidery needle

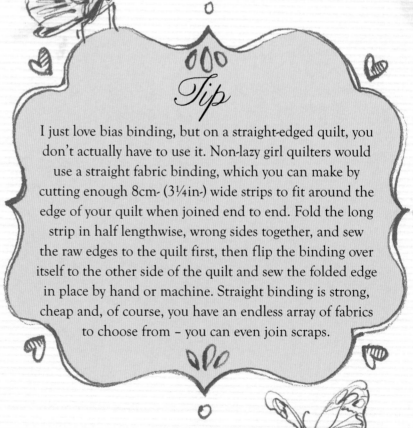

Tip

I just love bias binding, but on a straight-edged quilt, you don't actually have to use it. Non-lazy girl quilters would use a straight fabric binding, which you can make by cutting enough 8cm- (3¼in-) wide strips to fit around the edge of your quilt when joined end to end. Fold the long strip in half lengthwise, wrong sides together, and sew the raw edges to the quilt first, then flip the binding over itself to the other side of the quilt and sew the folded edge in place by hand or machine. Straight binding is strong, cheap and, of course, you have an endless array of fabrics to choose from – you can even join scraps.

THE CRAFTY MINX AT HOME

INSTRUCTIONS

1. Start by cutting out three sections of floral print – these will be the centrepieces of your blocks. They don't need to be the same size – in fact, they look better mismatched – but it's probably better if they're cut from the same piece of fabric, even if you use different areas of the print. If using smaller prints than the ones used here, or if you're aiming to create a large quilt, try cutting out five centrepieces instead (an odd number of arrangements always look better than an even number). Lay them out on the floor; these will form the uniting theme of your quilt. I have used floral pieces myself.

2. Take old and new fabrics (about seven to nine different colours and prints, more if you wish) and measure up before cutting in straight lines along the selvedge. Flip over and cut along other selvedge line as well. You may wish to fold the fabric over on itself a couple of times and use a rotary cutter to save time.

3. Cut 5–8cm- (2–3in-) wide strips of each fabric (vary the widths), and lay them out until you're happy with the effect. Small prints look better placed with larger ones and colours will sing when separated by a contrasting tone. With right sides facing each other, start sewing strips together until you have a 30–35cm- (12–14in-) wide piece of patchworked fabric. Press the fabric, but don't chop off the uneven lengths at the bottom, as these will come in handy later.

4. Lay your patchwork fabric on the cutting mat and use a rotary cutter and quilter's rule to cut random pieces crosswise, that is, across the joined strips. Cut squares, rectangles, triangles, whatever. The aim is to build a collection of fabric scraps around the floral centrepiece blocks without making it look too considered. The more haphazard the better, but keep in mind that different colours and print-sizes generally look best next to each other. Sew strips, squares and triangles of your string-pieced fabric to the centrepieces with a simple straight-stitch seam.

5. Don't fret too much about wonky seams. Keep the iron on, and press your patchwork flat as you add each piece. Snipping off loose threads now saves time later and keeps things neat.

6 When your three centrepiece blocks are complete, lay them on the floor and play until you're happy with the overall result, then start adding larger pieces of fabric around them. If a square or rectangle looks too understated on its own, try cutting down the middle or off-centre before sewing a strip of string-piecing to the middle. Keep in mind that you eventually need to sew the completed blocks together into one piece and that it is easiest to do this along straight lines, but don't stress too much – remember, you can always trim the edges into straight lines when you're ready.

7 When your quilt centre is complete, find a neutral fabric to sew around the border to make up the finished size; a monochrome colour or natural linen will frame the patchwork well and tone down any 'busyness'. Add leftover portions of string-piecing to the border to extend the linen, or just to add interest. Set the quilt top aside.

8 Iron and lay out your backing sheet, wrong side up, and cover with batting. Finally, add your quilt top, right side up. Using lots of safety pins, start pinning the layers together from the centre outwards, making sure all three layers are as flat as possible while pinning through.

9 Chop off any excess fabric from the backing sheet and Quilt-Light before using your machine to sew around all four edges. (If you have used a batting that is thicker than Quilt-Light, you should leave the excess backing and batting extending around the edges, and you should quilt the layers together first, then chop off the excess, before adding the binding last of all. This is because when you quilt through a thicker batting, it can pull up the fabric more than you think, leaving a backing sheet that is too small.)

10 Choose bias binding at this stage by taking your quilt top along to a haberdashery: it's not until now that you'll be able to tell which colour or print works best with all the different elements. Choose a colour that is under-represented overall but seems to work. For a quilt that pops, steer clear of anything too tasteful or matchy-matchy.

11 Stitch the binding to the back of the quilt first, allowing enough at each corner to make neat folds, then fold the remaining edge of the binding to the front, enclosing the raw edges of your quilt, and stitch it in place.

12 Now it's time to hand-quilt the layers together. You can have your quilt professionally machine-quilted to achieve the traditional squiggly or straight lines all over, but hand-quilting or embroidery will make it look more homespun and handmade. Use threads in a rainbow of colours to pick out prints and flower petals, and add appliqué or fabric yoyos (see instructions, page 62) for decoration as you see fit. To keep the back of the quilt neat, when you start a new thread, make a knot on the wrong side, then give your needle a gentle but firm tug to pull the knot through the backing, so that it is hidden between the layers. Take a small backstitch to keep the end secure, then continue.

Use all manner of interesting vintage curios for modern and quirky flower vessels

Blooming gorgeous

Vintage vessels fit for re-use as intriguing and unusual vases abound in flea markets and charity stores alike. Think pretty teacups, votive candle holders, bowls, jugs, an Edwardian silver ice bucket or waterproof tins. Even old Italian drink bottles, science beakers or '60s ceramic curios grouped in a well-arranged display can look loads better than your average traditional vase-with-flowers display. Create a floral tableau, comprised of garden-picked blooms and greenery, or single stems picked up on an early morning jaunt to the markets.

For our wedding we made all the flower arrangements ourselves (or at least my mother-in-law, her posse of girlfriends and I did) with blooms from their country farm in England as well as those bought at a local flower market. These were displayed in jam jars, crystal bowls and all sorts of different items such as royalty-printed teacups and tins. It looked really quirky and original displaying them down the centre of our banquet trestle tables, and so much more interesting than super-tasteful displays from a professional florist.

Stairway to heaven
bookcase

One of the most alluring aspects of a vintage object is re-imagining the ways in which it can be repurposed. Take your find out of context, pop it in a new one, and you've got a totally fresh-looking item to adorn the home and subvert expectations. It's quirky, original and just plain fun.

This ladder-cum-bookcase is my friend Sara's idea – it's a clever one and works so well in homes where space and storage are at a premium. Prop or mount it against a wall and play with displays. Try colour coding book spines or breaking up a solid bookcase with zen vases or curios arranged prettily on alternating rungs. Hang an old wooden puppet, silk roses, stiff tulle tutu or other atmospheric item from its side and presto, you've got yourself a compelling art installation.

THE CRAFTY MINX *AT HOME*

MATERIALS NEEDED

- Cool old wooden ladder with flat rungs, preferably covered in authentic paint splats – try a flea market or put the word out to tradie friends about what you're looking for

- Nails or screws – two for each rung of the ladder

- Hammer or screwdriver

- Wire

- String or cord

- Scissors

- Measuring tape

- Wire cutters

- Long strips of fabric or ribbon, to cover top step and sides (optional)

INSTRUCTIONS

1 Decide where you're going to place your ladder first, and then either lean it against the wall or attach at a semi-permanent angle. To do this, place a nail or screw in the wall on either side of the top step, wrap a length of wire around its front and wind the wire around nails until secured. I would recommend doing this if you have small children (and especially toddlers) at home.

2 Insert a small screw or nail about 10cm (4in) above each rung on the sides of the ladder, on those rungs where you'll be displaying books. It's a good idea to figure out your rough final arrangement of objects first.

3 Place books of the size and variety you'll be displaying on the rungs and measure how far they extend forwards from each rung. You want to place them roughly in the middle, to avoid falling forwards or backwards too easily.

4 Use your measuring tape to figure out the length of cord needed for the width of each rung, and cut to size with scissors.

5 Wrap cord several times around screw or nail on either side. Repeat for each rung – easy.

Tip

If your second-hand ladder is just plain grotty (rather than covered in arty paint splatters) try applying a full coat of paint or even better, wrapping ribbons or torn fabric around the sides and top step first. Stepladders also look great given this treatment, and work well repurposed as nifty bedside tables.

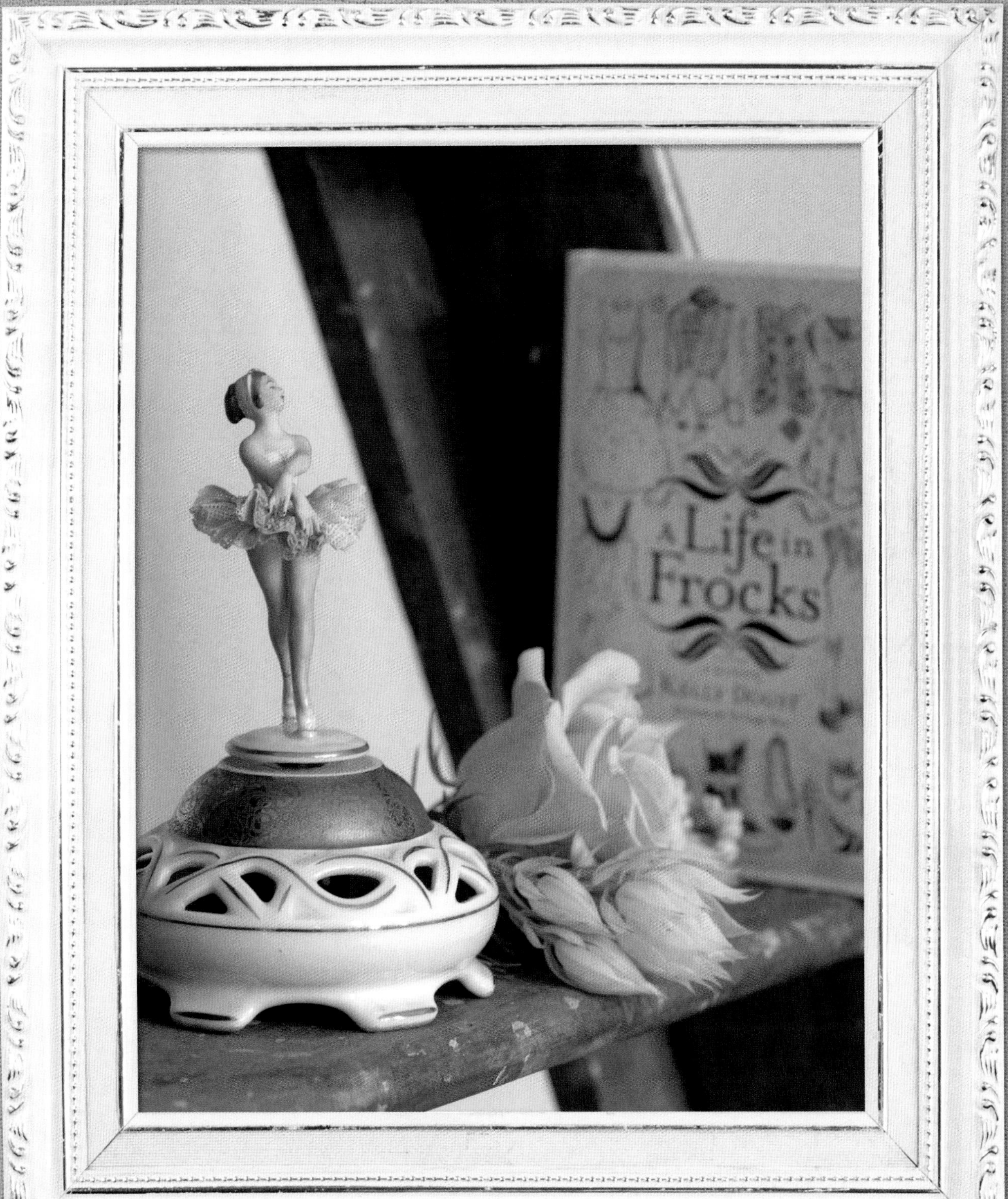
A Life in Frocks

Fantasy prints strike a chord in the bedroom

Romance never dies
wall hanging

This has to be one of the thriftiest, yet most striking ways to decorate the walls of your home: choose any fabric design that makes you happy and turn it into a framed canvas. Remarkably easy to do yourself, it's an inexpensive solution compared to buying an original artwork, more inspired than buying a print, and can inject a room with breathtakingly original chic. And nowhere more so than in the bedroom, where fantasy prints strike a chord.

MATERIALS NEEDED

- Wooden frame, available from any art supplies shop. The best are made from good-quality wood, with tongue and groove corners that fit into each other with a little help from a hammer tap
- Fabric to fit the frame – enough to cover the surface, sides and an extra few centimetres (an inch) to tuck neatly out of sight against the wall. A metre (1⅛yd) provides a wonderful canvas to gaze upon and fits well above most beds
- Iron
- Staple gun and staples

INSTRUCTIONS

1 Iron your fabric flat, right side down.

2 Place your frame over the fabric, then fold up the edges of one side and staple along the edge at 5–8cm (2–3in) intervals.

3 When you get to a corner, fold the fabric carefully around the edge like you would if you were wrapping a gift, then staple in place.

4 Keep going until you've finished all four sides, and your piece will be ready to hang.

The Boudoir

GUSSIED UP, VINTAGE STYLE

Boudoir [boo-dwahr, -dwaur]: A boudoir is a lady's private bedroom, sitting room or dressing room. The term derives from the French verb 'bouder', meaning 'to pout'.

Clever Virginia Woolf was right: every woman needs a room of one's own. Make mine a generous walk-in robe with large sash window and elaborate dressing table, bathed in soft natural light. Throw in a chaise longue and Louis XV-style side table for manoeuvring into towering heels with comfort or escaping with a cup of tea and an engaging novel, and decorate with feminine abandon in shades of blush, dusty blue and burnished metallic, set against simple, elegant French grey or eggshell. Keep the mood serene for your very own slice of heaven, add a bouquet of overblown roses for natural *parfum*, and let the fashion do the talking. A girl can dream.

The dressing room is the perfect place to procrastinate over a bevy of shoes and frocks and bags and jewels for myriad effects, and is ideally so large as to accommodate a host of girlfriends presiding over a clothing swap, wardrobe cull or simply a natter. One must emerge, eventually, for sustenance and other duties, but there's no need to rush. This female erogenous zone rewards patience.

Create a charming and transporting domain adorned with reclaimed furniture, clothing, jewels, feathers and other cleverly repurposed vintage items. Then give yourself space to move about and simply marinate.

The world can wait …

THE HUMBLE DRESSING TABLE

Common knowledge has it that these feminine fancies originated in France in the 18th century, but records of tables where ladies attended to their 'toilet' date back to at least the 17th century (and probably even earlier). Simple affairs to begin with, dressing tables were designed for keeping bits and bobs on and as part of matching bedroom suites – a popular purchase in Victorian and Edwardian times. Most pairings have been split up over time, though, as significant estates have been liquidated and dealers scattered them to the four winds.

The dressing table as a carved or painted lovely can still be found in museums and stately homes throughout Europe, with charming examples in the style of the day, such as Chinoiserie, very popular in the mid-18th century, following a fascination with anything Chinese in flavour and kitted out with faux-ebonised bamboo, black, red, green or gilt lacquer and intricate mother-of-pearl inlays. Other collectible styles sport neo-classical features when fashions of the time borrowed heavily from the antique. Ornate swags, wreaths, columns and beautiful symmetry all play their part in the creation of classic dressing tables of earlier eras.

Comparisons of English and French furniture are always interesting, but dressing tables of the 18th century particularly reveal the cultural differences of both countries at the time. In Georgian England, furniture was very masculine, so dressing tables resembling a kneehole desk or lowboy, often made from plain mahogany, were the norm. More exciting versions existed, that boasted a breakfront (rather than a straight piece from left to right) or line of inlaid timber, such as satinwood, known as 'stringing', but in essence, they were very blokey. By contrast, 18th-century

French cabinet-makers produced a diverse range of pieces for the dressing room with wonderful names such as Coiffeuse or Poudreuse and Table à Toilette, with typically slender cabriole legs, rather than the heavy kneehole flanked by chunky drawers. The French get my vote for bedroom elegance, hands down.

The most common Victorian dressing table, found in many antiques store or auction houses, is usually referred to as a 'Duchess', and is typically made from mahogany or cedar with a mirror sitting above a curvaceously shaped top. The arrangement often includes a single mirror set atop a dressing table, but occasionally is a hinged triptych so mirrors can be angled for a side-to-side view. Sets of drawers traditionally sit to either side, mounted upon a platform base. A lot of dressing tables from the art deco period and later (circa 1925–1960) have survived, often in rounded shapes with big circular mirrors, and in interesting veneers, such as bird's eye maple.

Moving from the jazz age to the space age, they morph from looking like oversized Bakelite radios to the all-pervading kidney shape, resembling lunar landing craft with their sputnik legs, similar to the early black and white television sets. Cheaper versions made with poor materials are ten a penny and haven't lasted well at all, but decent items in good condition will always remain excellent examples of mid-century modern furniture.

After a few years of being cast out into the wilderness, Duchesses and their 20th-century equivalents are now becoming sought-after once again. This may be a fad or reaction against built-ins, or perhaps the trend represents our nostalgia for visiting our dear old grandmothers, who owned dressing tables topped with exciting jars and potions, and drawers full of costume sparklers, beads and baubles to explore. Long may the trend continue, in my opinion.

Goddess 101

The dressing table has well and truly hit its renaissance, ladies. Find out why Granny was so right about taking time out for an indulgent toilette ritual.

Salvage a grand old vintage dressing table from an auction house, sand back its scuffed surfaces or paint in rich, vibrant hues the shade of a plump '50s-era pout, and sit upon your matching stool like Little Miss Muffet, ready to work your makeup magic. Clever Misses with compact living spaces will find beguiling triptych mirrors to set atop a chest of drawers for toilette rituals of the on-the-run variety, and even a mirror in a quiet corner with a shelf nearby provides welcome time-out space for getting ready in a leisurely fashion – something the modern world deprives us of so often.

Source crystal bowls and vases to store jewels, hairpins and makeup brushes in, place pretty parfum bottles out on display, invest in a Mason Pearson bristle brush for tress perfection and add a padded cushion to a primping stool for your pampered derrière. It's the only way to leave the home in style, don't you know? Enter Aphrodite.

She's a tease
makeup case

In a hectic world, a gal needs to carve out some alone time to prepare herself for the day ahead. The ritual of getting dressed and 'putting on your face' is a womanly tradition to hold sacred. Feel serene and meditative while creating the perfect scarlet pout, and things somehow seem brighter, more exciting. Hallelujah and Amen.

A small length of oilcloth goes a long way for making zippered cases and coin purses for the home and last-minute gifts. My favourite kind comes from Cath Kidston in spriggy florals or polka dots. Lined with pretty cotton gingham, this makeup case looks as fetching as you do after a good primping session.

Go forth and captivate.

MATERIALS NEEDED

- 32 x 50cm (12½ x 20in) oilcloth fabric – Cath Kidston produces hardy oilcloth with the best take on vintage designs
- 32 x 50cm (12½ x 20in) cotton gingham in a contrasting colour
- 30cm (12in) zipper
- Sewing machine and thread
- Zipper foot

Tip

This case is the perfect size for fitting in most makeup items. Use clear ziplock bags to separate brushes from other cosmetics, or make a smaller version for your handbag by following the same instructions but reducing the height by 20cm (8in). Brushes will need the same length to avoid crushing bristles.

INSTRUCTIONS

1 Place your oilcloth and gingham, right sides together and edges matching, and centre the zipper between the two layers, along the 32cm (12½in) edge, with the teeth of one side of the zipper front facing against the right side of the oilcloth. Using a zipper foot, sew along edge through all three layers, close to the zipper teeth.

2 Take the bottom edge of the oilcloth and fold it back up on itself, right sides together, lining it up with the remaining edge of the zipper tape. Do the same with the gingham, so the zipper is sandwiched, as before, and sew along this second edge. Your zipper is inserted.

3 Open the zipper partway. Bring the right sides of the oilskin together, and the right sides of the gingham together, with the zipper in the centre. Fold the zip, so that the tape is towards the oilcloth and the teeth are facing towards the gingham. Allowing a 1cm (³⁄₈in) seam, stitch the sides of the bag, both oilcloth and lining, leaving a 10cm (4in) opening in the lining on one side only. Take care that you are stitching just outside the metal stops at each end of the zipper.

4 To create the boxed corners on the case's base, snip the seam allowance open at each bottom fold, so that the seam will open flat, and pull the sides into a triangle shape so that the seam aligns with the bottom fold. Run a ruler down the seam from the apex until the base of the triangle measures 6cm (2½in) across (3cm (¼in) on each side of seam) and rule a line across. Sew on this line, then trim away excess fabric. Repeat for remaining three corners.

5 Turn case right side out, fold under the raw edges of the gingham, and sew opening closed.

6 Tuck the gingham inside the oilcloth and presto, your case is done.

THE CRAFTY MINX *AT HOME*

Narcissus lives
mirror

When clocking up some serious time gazing at your reflection, you'll want
a pretty frame. A zingy pep of acid bright always puts one in the mood for
colourful strutting, or keep it simple and simply chic with a white gloss
finish. Release your inner peacock, honey (go on, you know you want to).

MATERIALS NEEDED

- One fabulous vintage mirror; go for old, trashed gilt-framed versions with ample curlicues, which are easy to find and look magic after a revitalising facelift
- Damp cloth
- Masking tape
- White undercoat
- Glossy topcoat in neon colour such as fuchsia, tangerine or electric blue. Or just plain white as I've used here. Avoid green, the colour of envy
- Paintbrush

INSTRUCTIONS

1 Give your vintage mirror a glam second life with a simple few coats of paint. Start by removing dust and dirt with a damp cloth, then stick masking tape around its inner edges, as close as possible to where the mirror meets the frame.

2 Apply an undercoat, and follow with two coats of topcoat, allowing each coat to dry completely before each application.

3 Gently remove the tape and use your nails or a knife to remove any leftover flecks.

4 Spray and shine, then gaze away to your heart's content. Did anyone ever tell you? You really are a looker.

THE FAIREST OF THEM ALL

The earliest mirrors on record were created in the days of the Greek and Roman Empires, and took the form of polished silver discs. These were reflective, but nothing like the highly polished surfaces we take for granted today. The modern mirror actually dates back to the late 17th and early 18th centuries, when mercury-backed glass was first developed. With glass-blown panes limited in size and mercury being a highly dangerous chap to handle, mirrors became highly prized and sought-after possessions: the bigger the mirror, the greater the wealth and status of its owner. And because size came with technical experience, specialist makers would experiment with flamboyant ornamentation (Trumeau, built-in, Cheval, for ceilings), wherever a reflection was needed.

But to mention ornamentation without mentioning the Venetian mirror would be criminal: widely available and still popular in today's market, the Venetian mirror is instantly recognisable for curvaceously shaped mirror pieces, which are used to frame and enhance its brilliance. The glass is acid etched, and scroll or fan shapes adorn a central piece (the fancier the better) and occasionally include inlaid gemstones. Other popular styles of the 18th and 19th centuries include porcelain-encrusted with rosebuds and the like (favoured by the Germans) and anything gilded or painted (a particular penchant of the French). Yet another example is the lovely Trumeau mirror, which features a panel containing part-mirror, part-painting.

Prior to modern manufacturing, mirrors really were prohibitively expensive to produce. 17th- and 18th-century craftsmen risked mercury poisoning, so when you see an antique piece that is to die for, it may well have been. Perhaps this explains the superstition surrounding carelessness with mirrors, and the 'bad luck' associated with breaking one. Childhood and Victorian literature often uses mirror as a narrative device (think Lewis Carroll or Oscar Wilde), and the Hall of Mirrors was a popular novelty pastime in the era. Artists, such as Jan van Eyck in the European Renaissance, used the mirror in portraits of his wealthy patrons, the Arnolfinis, and cheekily included his own reflection.

From simple styles to the more ornate, Europe still has the edge on mirror design. The best example of exquisite early mirrors has to be the Hall of Mirrors in the Château de Versailles. Designed by Mansart in the 1670s

as an ostentatious display of wealth by Louis XIV, it was also intended as a bit of a snub to Venice – widely considered to be the glass capital of Europe. A walk through this exquisite palace room is testament to the vast wealth of the French court. No wonder the starving masses cried *Revolution!* in response.

With the modernisation of manufacturing processes, the 20th century saw the mirror begin to be used in some very exciting ways. In fashion (who can forget that dress with the wing mirrors attached?), and in popular culture, by icons such as Elvis, or in disco balls, to name but a few. The mirror's possibility for kitsch seems never-ending, but so too is it a form of inspiration, with yet new designs being created every day.

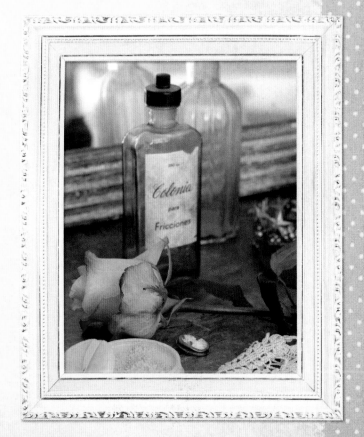

Keep it kawaii
tissue case

Forget about bling and all your hollow status symbols, lady. Indulge in tactile pleasures and hand-make to feed the soul instead. That's my idea of transcendental bliss, minus the Om.

This little number comes in handy at the dressing table and also makes ideal present material. Whip up a stack and store away for last-minute gifts. I tend to add one to a beribboned box of chocolates, cinema ticket and handmade card for a girlfriend on her birthday (or is an escapist film *sans* company just my idea of the perfect afternoon?)

MATERIALS NEEDED

- Pretty linen cloth or tea towel
- Contrasting bias binding – use up short scraps left over from other craft projects
- Scissors
- Sewing machine and thread
- Small pack of tissues

Rose Black Tea

NET WT. 2½ OZ.

*Forget about bling, lady ...
hand-make to feed the soul*

INSTRUCTIONS

1. Lay your tea towel flat, and find the prettiest image or spray of flowers to feature on the back of your case.

2. Pop the pack of tissues on top and chop around the outside, leaving a few centimetres' (an inch) seam allowance.

3. Repeat for the front, before cutting down the middle vertically – you should now have three separate pieces of fabric.

4. Take the bias binding and sew along the wrong side of each front piece for the opening.

5. Fold binding over the raw edge and sew flat on the right side.

6. Place the two top pieces on the bottom piece, with right sides facing out. Sew around all four sides, a few millimetres ($\frac{1}{8}$ in) in from the edge.

7. Turn wrong side out, clip the corners, and sew around all four sides again with the raw edges tucked inside to create a French seam.

8. Reverse a few times where the opening pieces meet at the top and bottom of the case for strength, turn right side out, *et voilà*.

Turn right side out …
et voilà

Tip

Collect crisp vintage linens for this project. Old tablecloths and tea towels, oftentimes never used, are printed in gorgeous brights and will be the perfect weight for tissue cases or small, pretty zippered cases. They're also widely available in flea markets and thrift stores.

THE CRAFTY MINX *AT HOME*

Spanish Steps
necklace

How I love elements of traditional Spanish style – matadors and dancing girls, and the drama of red, black and white. A lacy collar or impeccably tailored bolero sends me weak in the knees, let alone a combative glare and arched brow glimpsed beneath a matador hat brim. *Ole!* Gold braid or frogging, tiered silk ruffles, satin-edged tuxedo pants and a coltish nobility: the look has such theatre, passion and romance. Such Old World beauty, *si*?

I'm always collecting bits and pieces that I find impossible to leave behind, even with no fixed purpose in mind (hard as I try otherwise and, yes, in contrast to advice you'll find earlier in this book). All the items used to create this bib-style necklace were stored in a box full of such fancies. In a moment of discovery they came together, as if of their own accord. I merely sewed them into place.

MATERIALS NEEDED

- Lacy bib, collar or fabric in the shape of the bodice overleaf. A Peter Pan-style collar works equally well. If you can't find one, make your own from a layer or two of heavyweight vintage linen or damask, and finish the edges with a thin strip of lace with the pattern shown here
- Salvaged chandelier crystals, broken antique brooches or elegant pearl buttons
- A couple of metres' (a couple of yards') worth of black grosgrain ribbon
- A length of antique lace
- Pins
- Needle and thread

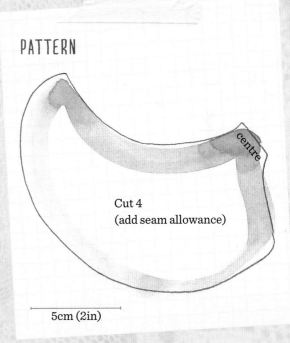

PATTERN

centre

Cut 4
(add seam allowance)

5cm (2in)

INSTRUCTIONS

1 Allowing an ample amount of ribbon for tying a bow at the nape of your neck (about 35cm (14in) should do it), pin grosgrain ribbon to the top left edge of bib.

2 Layer lace over remaining grosgrain, and create small layers by folding down and over, then down and over again, until you reach the centre. Pin into place as you go.

3 Leave a further 20cm (8in) before chopping lace and ribbon at an angle.

4 Repeat on right side edge of the bib.

5 Using small stitches with off-white thread to match the lace, sew the ruffled layers into place in the centre of each layer (rather than at the top, which will make it sit too flat).

6 When you've finished sewing, fold the trailing ribbons and lace in the centre (as if to tie a bow) but pin down before knotting.

7 Cut a small piece of ribbon – about 5cm (2in) long – and fold over the two sides of the bow in its middle.

8 Sew into place with black thread.

9 Attach chandelier crystals, broken brooch or pearl buttons vertically down the centre of the bib or three pearl buttons in a row, which works a treat. *Iestá acabado* (he's finished).

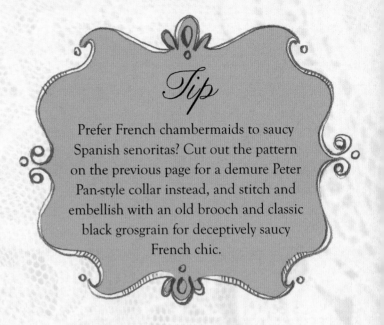

Tip

Prefer French chambermaids to saucy Spanish senoritas? Cut out the pattern on the previous page for a demure Peter Pan-style collar instead, and stitch and embellish with an old brooch and classic black grosgrain for deceptively saucy French chic.

Hello, Texas
camellia corsage

Why Texas? Because this corsage comes straight out of the super-sized state. Make a statement on the lapel of your smartest blazer with a blooming camellia brooch, or glam up a favourite frock or tote with this gorgeous floral addition. Too fresh.

MATERIALS NEEDED

- Pencil
- A4 paper
- Scissors (paper and dressmaker's)
- Iron
- Vliesofix or double-sided appliqué webbing
- Vintage silk scarf or frock offcuts – a damaged, stained piece with a beautiful print will be perfect for chopping up
- Linen or cotton to stabilise the silk
- 100% wool felt
- Needle
- Pearl embroidery thread
- Ribbon
- Button
- Sew-on brooch back or safety pin

PATTERN

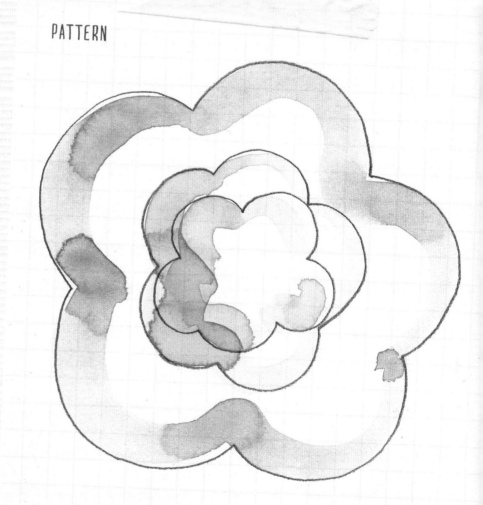

INSTRUCTIONS

1. Use a pencil to draw the basic flower pattern freehand onto paper at your desired corsage size. Then draw 2–5 additional flowers (depending on the size of the first), each approximately 1cm (³⁄₈ in) smaller than the last. Number the flower patterns in order, and cut out with scissors.

2. Iron Vliesofix to the silk scarf by first ironing the scarf flat, right side down, then placing the Vliesofix on top, paper side facing upwards. Iron paper side on a low setting (or with a pressing cloth, to protect the silk) until the fabric has bonded to the Vliesofix. Allow to cool.

3. Place the odd-numbered flower shapes on top of the Vliesofix's paper side, and trace around each.

4. Cut out, remove the backing paper and place on top of the linen. Iron on a low setting until the two layers are bonded. Then cut around the flowers again.

5. For the even-numbered flower shapes, place on felt and cut around the flower patterns. Use a running stitch to sew around the edges of each.

6. Place each layer on top of the larger layer before it, with petals intersecting, to form our camellia-inspired flower. Place aside.

7. Loop ribbon over on itself several times to create the floral centre. Hold in place tightly with thumb and forefinger.

8. Take needle and thread, and stitch through ribbon then the layers of the flower before threading the button to the top layer. Thread through a few more times until it feels properly secured, then make a few more stitches at the back for strength.

9. Add your brooch back or safety pin with needle and thread – you're done.

BIRD LOVE

Create a bird brooch the same way, following the instructions and using this bird shape instead. To add felt, simply sew a running stitch through both layers, then chop around the shape, leaving 5mm (¼in) beyond the stitching for your birdie's border.

PATTERN

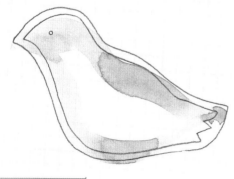

5cm (2in)

THE CRAFTY MINX AT HOME

*Wear your handmade
adornments with pride*

Tip

Gather favourite scraps of vintage or reclaimed fabric together and create added yoyos (for instructions, see page 60). Bright silks, cotton and linen look best on this summer-weight scarf.

We're having a heatwave
scarf

I live in scarves. In winter, woolly versions are just the ticket for protecting neck and chest from icy winds. And in summer-weight cottons or gauzy silk, they're eternally chic when added to a casual ensemble. Artfully knotted or strewn, scarves also double as pretty decoration for shopping totes or favourite corners of the home, and cover up bad hair days.

Add a form of freestyle decoration to yours with a bright visible running stitch, row of pompoms or pretty fabric yoyos. Hark at you, Miss Boho Fabulous.

MATERIALS NEEDED

- 2m (2¼yd) cotton or linen in a pale colour that flatters your skin tone. Hold fabric against your face before buying (use a hand mirror and natural light – even if you have to leave the store to view properly). To save on cost with new fabric, you might want to sew pieces together to make a 2m (2¼yd) length
- 2m (2¼yd) cotton or linen in a contrasting shade
- Dressmaker's scissors
- Sewing machine and thread
- Needle
- Pearl embroidery thread
- Small scraps of fabric for yoyo decorations (optional, see page 62 for instructions)
- Row of tiny pompoms or lace for ends (optional), available from a haberdashery

INSTRUCTIONS

1. Make sure your pale fabric is the correct width for a scarf by chopping to desired size – lay out a favourite scarf on the floor first to use as your 'pattern'. Mine measures 2m long x 40cm wide (2¼yd x 16in).

2. Cut the ends at an angle, as I've done here.

3. Lay pale fabric over contrasting fabric, right sides together, and stitch together on the machine around all four sides, leaving a 5cm (2in) gap at the very end.

4. Clip the corners with scissors.

5. Turn right side out, using your fingers to pop out the corners.

6. Turn under the raw edges and sew opening closed.

7. Use embroidery thread in a bright shade to sew a running stitch around all four edges, making small knots at the beginning and end on the darker side of the scarf.

8. Add a decorative yoyo, or a row of mini pompoms or lace, if you fancy, to either end.

Bit-part in your life
cameo armoire

Cameos and Wedgwood-style silhouettes will always be considered classic and unabashedly romantic. In plain black and white, silhouettes also look masculine and Old Worldly, redolent of low-lit, wood-panelled libraries covered in maps, and filled with chesterfields and vellum-bound books. They therefore work well in decoration for shared bedrooms, or better than the purely girly kind, at least.

I bought this antique wardrobe for very little at a flea market, and had it home-delivered. When I told the dealer that I was planning to paint it a French-inspired blue-grey, he immediately regretted selling it to me, and wanted to buy it back. But the original dark-stained wood was crying out for a makeover – especially when I noticed how small it made our bedroom look. With the original skeleton key missing, he wouldn't have had much success anyway, and so finally agreed to let me keep it.

There are many pieces of second-hand furniture not worth the investment of time or money for an overhaul. Those made from MDF and veneer that originally arrived in a flat pack, for a start. But also old, badly damaged pieces without any real integrity or charm to begin with. This turn-of-the-century item had both in spades, including slightly worn-down doors that feel lovely to handle. I found a stack of old keys in a used furniture store I visit frequently, and the last one in the box worked (after almost 50 failed attempts).

Too small to contain many clothes, this armoire stores my accessories collection and anything that doesn't require hanging: 40 or so pairs of shoes, sunglasses, several handbags and various tops, jeans and underwear. I added shelving on one side, which makes claiming shoes much easier than if all the pairs were stacked on top of each other, and I bought storage boxes to fit smaller items, such as socks, bras and negligées.

Our homes fill up quickly ... don't rush into buying large items of furniture

PATTERN

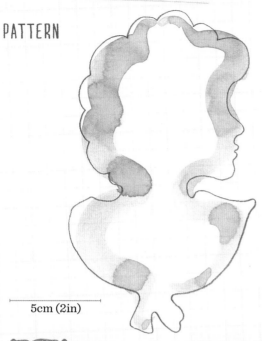

5cm (2in)

- Fab old wooden wardrobe
- Sandpaper and block
- Cloth
- Masking tape
- 1 litre (34fl oz) white undercoat paint
- 2 litres (68fl oz) grey matt finish paint; I prefer environmentally friendly versions, such as this Porter's standard wall paint, which is so safe you can sleep in the same room that night without getting a headache from the fumes
- Tester-sized pot of black matt paint
- Medium-sized paintbrush for applying undercoat and topcoat, plus smaller artist's brush or stencil brush for the cameo detail (to copy the silhouette I've used, blow up the pattern here on a photocopier)
- A4 paper
- Craft knife
- Beeswax
- Rag for applying beeswax
- Additional wooden shelves – preferably made from reclaimed wood – if you choose, plus a hammer and nails

INSTRUCTIONS

1 Sand your entire wardrobe with a piece of sandpaper and block, and dust off with a damp cloth.

2 Cover any fixtures or fittings, such as hinges and handles, with masking tape, or unscrew and place aside if you're really concerned about covering with paint.

3 Apply a coat or two of undercoat, and 2–3 topcoats, allowing for each coat to dry completely before each application.

4 Draw desired silhouette on a piece of paper and use a craft knife to cut out for your cameo stencil.

5 Attach stencil to the centre panel with masking tape, then paint with a sparing amount of matt black paint, using your brush with a dabbing motion. Do not load your brush with too much paint or it will seep under the edges.

6 When all paint is completely dry, rub beeswax over the entire piece – too easy.

Tip

Don't rush into buying large pieces of furniture. Homes fill up very quickly and you're better off going without until you find the right item to pour your substantial efforts into reinventing. It also means you'll replace things less often. Buy once and with the intention of buying for life, if you can.

BRING OUT THE BIG GUNS

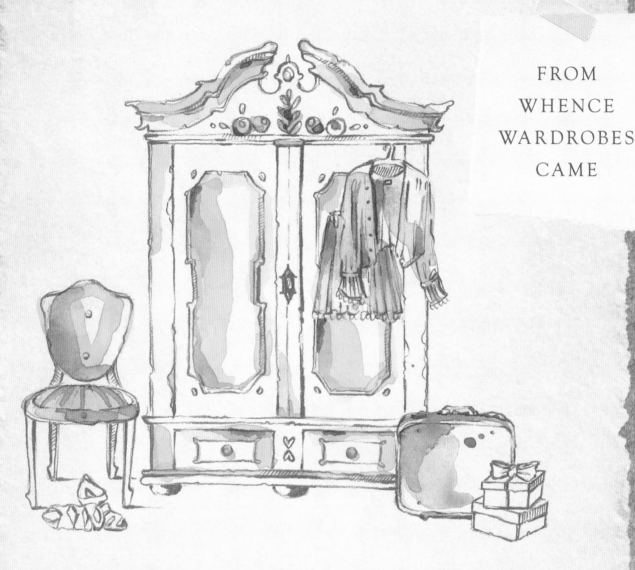

FROM WHENCE WARDROBES CAME

The term 'armoire' stems from the armoury or gun cupboard, where important things in the household were kept safe and secure. They were originally built to store firearms rather than killer frocks, but the past 500 years or so have seen many changes in how we revere and store clothes (and guns); hence its evolution.

The wardrobe or armoire as we know it became ubiquitous with the growth of fashion. Georgians, in particular, spent a fantastic amount of time getting ready, on occasion changing outfits up to five times a day. There were tea gowns, driving suits, evening gowns, hunting attire and myriad items to accommodate the

164

leisure-filled lives of the landowning gentry, so wardrobes grew to reflect this, with cavernous, Narnia-style versions, owned largely by the wealthy.

In Europe, many different types of timbers and fruitwoods were felled to create domestic wardrobes, with softwood species, such as cedar and camphorwood, employed to deter the little marauders, moths and silverfish. The harder the wood (or technically, the denser the wood), the more problems arose. Walnut and mahogany provided very tasty treats indeed for pests, so were best avoided in the interests of longevity.

The difference between provincial carving and metropolitan precision was as night versus day: metal strappings and locks, first used for utility, soon developed into decorative features and, as always, those created by the best craftspeople fetched the highest prices. Marquetry, a widely used decorative technique, involved the inlay of woods or precious material into the carcass, and exotic timbers were often used sparingly for exquisite patterns. A geometric approach, commonly seen in French pieces, parquetry used kingwood to create a chevron appearance. Other popular types of decoration included paintwork, which was both colourful and scenic, Ormolu or gilt mounts, and metal doors. Occasionally, all types of decoration were employed in the one piece, making a boomingly loud statement – the Russians were very fond of this approach.

These days plainer or even beaten-up provincial pieces tend to be hotly contested at auction, although this trend is battling the current mood for downsizing. Wardrobes have recently fallen from favour due to another shift in fashion – the penchant for built-ins has made the traditional standalone unnecessary. Countless armoires have been dismantled or repurposed over the years, and it is unlikely they'll be produced again in such numbers, but they may well become popular when the price for good period pieces outweighs the temptation to use reclaimed timber for other projects.

Really well-carved and attractive armoires will always find a home – even if they take up half the bedroom. Popular shabby chic finishes brighten up the dour, imposing look of those originally stained to a dark brown or black, and many of us now use them in different rooms for storing items other than clothes, such as televisions or bedding.

Lo, it's the little one

CHILDISH WHIMSY

Decorating a child's room is never done – from the time they're born to the time they scarper off into the world – and nor should it be. More so than in any other room of the home, furniture and style will always be evolving with the whims of constant change and growth. Bedrooms for small people and teens should be anything but serious; there's a whole lifetime ahead for that. Now's the time to indulge in fantasy, fun and youthful experimentation.

Anyone with a child will be aware that their tastes tend to run at odds with your own (hardly surprising, given they're entirely separate individuals; it's hard to remember that sometimes, as a parent) and those tastes are constantly changing. Tricky, when you're trying to create a thoroughly attractive home. Gently guide with your own ideas, but allow children and, especially, teenagers the freedom to inject ample personality of their own. Otherwise they'll only revolt one day and paint the walls black – either literally or figuratively.

Return home with arms full of furniture and heads full of ideas

From an early age, set the scene for creativity and daydreaming, with reclaimed items sourced from the unlikeliest of places. Inspire budding imaginations by involving them in artsy recycling, and ask for help choosing colours and favourite pieces to feather a formative nest. Make each project a collaborative one, and encourage them to seek inspiration everywhere; from a leaf or make-believe place, to the texture of sea glass or the interesting patina on an old watering can, while considering the same yourself.

Come council cleanup day, take young ones in hand on a tour of the local neighbourhood to see if there's any treasure to be found amongst the trash and, soon as they're old enough, on early-morning flea market or garage sale adventures. Return home with arms full of furniture and heads full of ideas. Prod your children to think laterally, and pass on the 'make do and mend' ethos to another generation, a not-insubstantial gift. And if you have any talent for woodworking, upholstery, painting, knitting, crochet or any other special skills, share that as well.

Oh, for the luxury of such days together, creating memories for the years to come.

Barn owl *doorstop*

Why not create a set of guardians to watch over your children in your absence?

I've appointed Monkey, Dog and a host of other small inanimate creatures to play sentry in my daughter's bedroom, both to remind her how much I love her and to keep her company while she sleeps. They also have the added bonus of being fun toys to play with during daylight hours and double up as useful homeware items, such as this Barn Owl doorstop which guards the entrance to her room.

The majestic barn owl welcomes all ye who enter.

MATERIALS NEEDED

- Random scraps of fabric and remnant upholstery cuts, enough to construct the front, back and base of this roughly 20cm- (8in-) tall, 10cm- (4in-) wide doorstop and for added details, such as face, wings and ears

- Dressmaker's chalk

- Scissors

- Rice, for weight and to fill

- Polyester fibrefill to stuff the remainder and provide added pouf beneath the wings

- Sewing machine and thread

- Pins

- Needle

INSTRUCTIONS

1 On a table, lay out the fabric you've chosen for your owl doorstop's front (neutral works best for adding colourful detail), right side up, and draw a rough owl shape with your chalk. Cut out with your scissors, remembering to leave some seam allowance.

2 Place the cut-out shape on another piece of backing fabric, facing right side down this time, and use as a pattern to create the back.

3 Sew or embroider details, such as button eyes, belly, face and ears to the front piece of fabric.

4 With right sides together, sew around the side and top edges of the owl shape, leaving the base open.

5 Leaving the two sewn-together pieces still inside-out, use your fibrefill to roughly fill the 'pillow' created, and stand it on top of a third piece of remnant fabric.

6 Use chalk to draw around the circular outside of the base and cut out, adding 1.5cm (½in) seam allowance all round. Remove stuffing and place aside.

7 Pin and sew the base to the 'pillowcase', leaving a 5cm (2in) gap open.

8 Turn right side out, poking out the edges with a chopstick or your fingers.

9 Fill with fibrefill again, to begin with, and then with rice until the doorstop is almost full and heavy enough to stand upright against the door by itself.

10 Sew the opening together by hand with needle and thread, using small, firm stitches – you don't want the rice escaping.

11 Sew wing shapes together for each side, leaving an opening for stuffing gently with fibrefill and a chopstick, for added pouf. Sew up the opening and attach to the owl. You're done.

THE CRAFTY MINX AT HOME

Temples of delight
crochet flower garlands

If you want to bring an authentic vintage, handmade feel to your home, consider introducing a spot of crochet. Collect blankets, pot holders and tea cosies, or make your own with delicious woolly yarns throughout winter and cool-to-touch cottons in summer. Display proudly and use every day.

Carelessly cut cloth strips, felt or wool pompoms, triangular bunting, paper streamers and doilies or trailing ribbons tied or sewn to string all make gorgeous garlands for a child's room and special celebrations. This is a garland designed to be treasured, kept and handed down, with love.

Carry all the materials needed in your handbag to make its flower shapes while on the train or waiting in line, even during afternoon tea with a friend. If you can manage a few each day, you'll find it finished in no time.

MATERIALS NEEDED

- 1–2 skeins or balls of 4-ply variegated wool, such as these delicious, digitally coloured 'Koigu' merino yarns from Japan, or 'Jitterbug' yarn from Wales (so yummy-looking … couldn't you just eat them up?), for a 5m- (5½yd-) long garland
- 1 ball of 4-ply wool, in a contrasting colour for the flower's centre (optional)
- 3.25mm crochet hook (US size D, UK size 10)
- Small scissors
- Wool needle

Sometimes the back of a crocheted item looks more interesting and intricate than its front.

These garlands look dear looped over a
bedhead or pinned to the picture rails.
Always be on the lookout for unusual
children's furniture, such as this rare pink
and white Formica-topped dressing table,
which I bought in immaculate condition
at the annual Fifties Fair, held at Sydney's
historic Rose Seidler House.

INSTRUCTIONS

For each metre (1⅛yd) of garland, you will need to make 10 flowers. After completing the first flower, crochet additional flowers together (see below) or stitch them together at the end with same-coloured wool. It is easier to crochet them together in the first place, but if you want to make flowers while out and about, sew them up later so you won't have to carry the entire garland around with you.

Abbreviations:

ch = chain; dc = double crochet; dtr = double treble; rep = repeat; sl st = slip stitch; tr = treble

FLOWER

1. Using either variegated yarn or contrasting colour yarn (if you want your flower to have a different-coloured centre), crochet 5ch, sl st in 5th ch from hook, making a ring.

2. Round 1: 3ch (counts as 1tr), 11tr in ring, join with sl st in 1st tr space (12tr).

3. Round 2: 4ch (counts as 1tr, 2ch), *1tr in next tr space, 2ch; rep from * to end of round, join with sl st in 1st tr space (12tr).

4. If you have used a contrast yarn for flower centre, break off yarn and join in new colour for next 2 petal rounds.

5. Round 3: 3ch (counts as 1tr), (1tr, 8ch, 1tr) in 1st tr space; *2tr in next tr space, 1tr, 8ch, 1tr in next tr space; rep from * another 4 times; 1tr in last tr space, join with sl st to 1st tr space (6 x 8-ch loops).

6. Round 4: 1dc into 1st 8-ch loop, *10dtr into 1st 8-ch loop, 1dc into 2tr space; rep from * to end of round, join with sl st to start of first petal. Fasten off.

TO CROCHET FLOWERS TOGETHER

1. After the first flower is completed, align the petals of the completed flower with those of a subsequent flower and, in Round 5, on the last petal of the flower in progress, work 3dtr of the 10-dtr cluster, then work the next 4dtr through both the completed flower petal and the 8-ch loop of the working flower to join the edges, then work the final 3dtr of the 10-dtr cluster to complete the petal.

2. When garland is completed, use a wool needle to weave those loose threads back into the flowers until all are hidden.

Tip

Create a gorgeous brooch by making two flower shapes, placing one on top of the other and sewing together in the centre. Pull stitching tight to scrunch up petals for a finished flower shape, then add a safety pin at the back for this lovely decorative pin-on.

Wild oats *bag*

Almost too simple for words, this one. Collect used oat or grain bags and turn them into storage for trucks, dolls and toys on the go. Larger bags can be slung from low hooks attached to the wall for clothes storage, and smaller versions make for a sweet girls' tote. Opt for cereals stored in calico sacks over the cardboard-boxed kind, and pop them away until ready to whip up a number of these super-cute recycled gifts in one go.

MATERIALS NEEDED

- Used calico oat sack
- Bias binding to finish open edges
- Length of pompom braid (optional)
- Sewing machine and thread
- Iron
- Length of cotton twill tape or sturdy canvas strap

INSTRUCTIONS

1 Turn your bag inside out and sew one side of bias binding around the inner edge of the opening.

2 Turn right side out, fold over bias binding and iron flat.

3 Insert a length of pompom braid, then sew bias flat around outer edge.

4 Add a length of cotton tape or sturdy canvas strap for the handle or handles before stitching in a square formation twice on each side for strength.

Tip

For a boy's version, use two lengths of cotton twill tape stitched to the back of the sack to create backpack-style straps instead. Add a button and buttonhole to the top, so stored items won't easily fall out.

THE CRAFTY MINX AT HOME

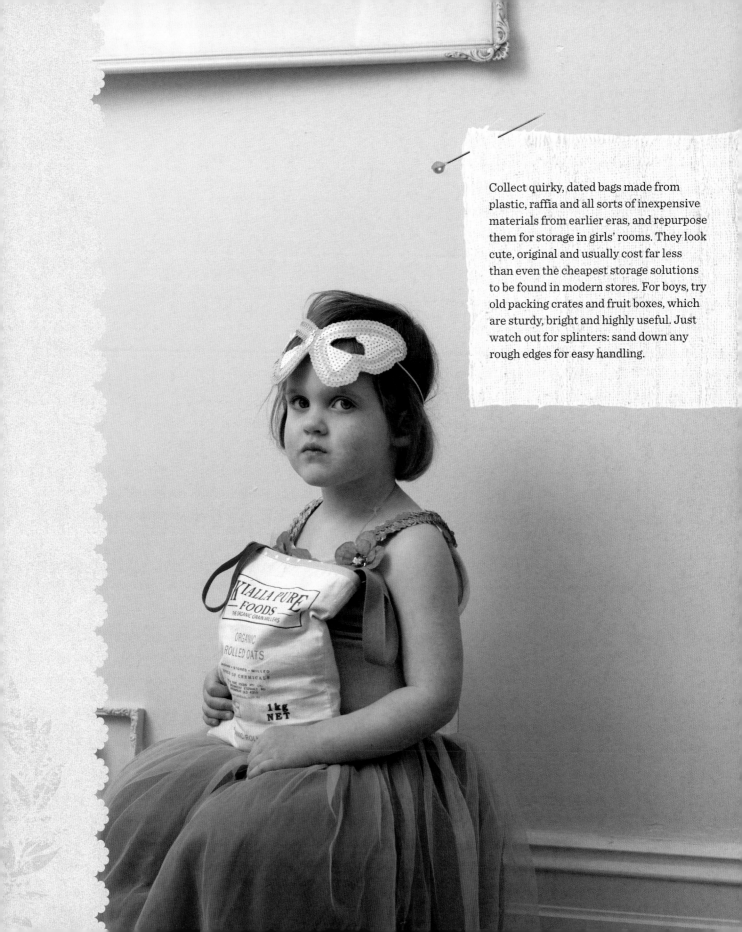

Collect quirky, dated bags made from plastic, raffia and all sorts of inexpensive materials from earlier eras, and repurpose them for storage in girls' rooms. They look cute, original and usually cost far less than even the cheapest storage solutions to be found in modern stores. For boys, try old packing crates and fruit boxes, which are sturdy, bright and highly useful. Just watch out for splinters: sand down any rough edges for easy handling.

Rococo-a-go-go *frames*

Amateur artists will revel in the importance given to early expressionist attempts with these ornate reclaimed frames. Stockpile a collection in different shapes and sizes, add a lick of paint, and mount in your child's room. Keep the artwork on high rotation for a constantly evolving look that is fresh and playful. Serious cardboard mounting and glass not required.

Buy unattractive prints in pretty vintage frames for the framing alone, and ditch the rest. For a whimsical effect, paint in wildly clashing colours or neon spray paint, placing your helper on spraying duty. For more muted chic, paint all the same colour in neutral black, grey or white and let colourful art do the talking.

MATERIALS NEEDED

- A collection of chipped and damaged rococo-style gilt frames
- Craft knife (strictly for grown-ups)
- Old newspaper
- Cloth and spray cleaner
- Old toothbrush
- White undercoat paint
- Gloss acrylic or neon spray paint (now's time to let them have all the fun)
- A selection of your child's favourite paintings or illustrations
- Paper scissors
- Three-pin picture hooks
- Hammer

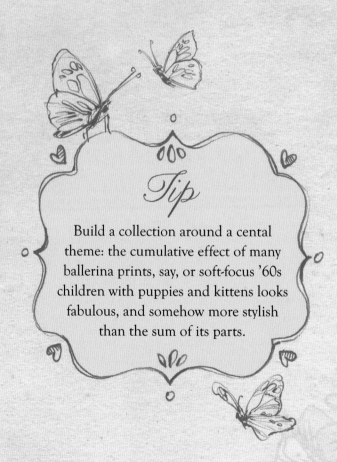

Tip

Build a collection around a cental theme: the cumulative effect of many ballerina prints, say, or soft-focus '60s children with puppies and kittens looks fabulous, and somehow more stylish than the sum of its parts.

178

*Artwork on high rotation
keeps a child's room
fresh and playful*

INSTRUCTIONS

1. Use your craft knife to cut away any masking tape, and remove each frame's backing. Pull out your unlovely prints and any cracked or broken glass, wrapping carefully in old newspaper before ditching in the bin.

2. Spray cleaner on frames and wipe away as much dust as possible, using an old toothbrush to work out reluctant dust bunnies from deep crevices.

3. Pick a sunny, still day to head outside, and use more newspaper to protect any ground surfaces. Lay out your frames and prepare with a white undercoat paint.

4. Finish frames with a variety of neon spray paints – the kind graffiti artists use. Your children will relish the chance to help out here. Or simply paint with whichever glossy acrylic shade takes your fancy.

5. Place paper artworks over the back of the frame with the art facing down and simply cut around with your scissors, leaving a 1–2cm ($^3/_8$–$^3/_4$ in) overlap for each picture to sit neatly behind its frame.

6. Secure with a couple of strips of masking tape at top and bottom of paper, or one on each corner.

7. When all your frames are ready to hang, play with various layouts on the wall until you're happy with the results and secure with three-pin picture hooks or even Blu tack – the frames should be fairly light without glass and backing, and such a carefree display will be easy to shift about on a whim.

THE CRAFTY MINX AT HOME

On the road
trunks and suitcases

The English comedian Daniel Kitson once performed a show called '66a Church Road – A Lament Made of Memories and Kept in Suitcases'. It's a monologue about his time spent renting a London house, and all the recollections tied up in the places we live. Both funny and full of pathos, it really made one think about the notion of home; how it's not just where the house is, and how we place so much importance upon material things both to ground and define us.

Adults love being at home surrounded by all our things and so do children, but it's a worthwhile reminder that we can be happy anywhere, and with very little. A house is just a shell, after all. It's the weight of memories that makes it a home and the people we share it with. Pass it on.

Old trunks and suitcases make inspired storage for children's bedrooms, suggesting trips to far-flung corners of the Earth – something to be encouraged, I think. Dust one off, add a pretty racing stripe, line it if you will and fill to the brim with favourite things before digging in. There you have it: a mini-adventure in a box.

MATERIALS NEEDED

- An old trunk or suitcase
- Damp cloth
- Vintage wallpaper or pretty wrapping paper
- Ruler
- Pencil
- Paper scissors
- Tacky craft glue
- Masking tape
- Paint and paintbrush; glossy red enamel is quite fetching, as is dusty pale blue
- Lavender sachet (to make your own, see page 265)

INSTRUCTIONS

1. Most old trunks and suitcases are fairly musty from years of storage in sheds and attics. To begin with, clean off any dust with a damp cloth and leave outside on a really sunny day to air out and properly dry.

2. To line with vintage wallpaper or pretty wrapping paper, use a ruler and pencil to jot down its internal measurements on all four sides and base. Add together, adding an extra half-centimetre (¼ in) or more just in case.

3. Cut out one large, cross-shaped piece of paper.

4. Carefully apply glue to its wrong side, making sure there are no large blobs of glue or missed areas.

5. Tuck inside case and smooth down.

6. Repeat steps 2–5 for the lid.

7. Close case and use masking tape to run straight lines down the centre of the case – these are your racing stripe outlines.

8. Paint inside taped areas and allow to dry. Three coats work best for an excellent finish.

9. Remove tape and store your cases in a haphazard stack – a variety of colours or tonal displays both look fetching.

Tip

My best tip for keeping a stylish home with children is to pop various collections of playthings in different boxes, and place them strategically around the house, much the way childcare centres do. They can go wild tearing one or two apart, but contents should go back in their box before all are opened. This keeps toys on high rotation and alleviates boredom, for there's always an element of surprise in digging out some fabulous, forgotten thing.

LAND AHOY: HAVE TRUNK, WILL TRAVEL

The history of the travel trunk is closely associated with the evolution of chests of drawers. In the 17th century, Italian and Portuguese seafarers took to carting their 'Cassone' with them on long boat journeys. Lighter, portable chests to keep one's possessions in, travel trunks or 'Steamer' trunks were the forerunner to the modern suitcase, and came in all shapes and sizes – from small hat boxes through to larger trunks with multiple compartments and flat tops for sliding under cabin beds and stacking, through to dome-topped or 'wardrobe' trunks.

The rise of travel for pleasure in the late Victorian era saw a great many of these items produced, and antique and vintage examples created by top manufacturers of the day still rival or exceed modern-day equivalents in price. The materials used were as varied as the passengers themselves, and range from the most basic to lavishly extravagant. Some were relatively simple affairs, and others had a whole range of compact, in-built features, such as hinged drawers and racks, depending on the extensiveness of the owner's wealth and wardrobe. Linings ranged from plain, thin paper to luxurious padded silk, similarly depending on the depth of an owner's pockets.

In later centuries, when reasons for sea travel were less about exploration and more about exploitation, a whole range of items referred to as 'Campaign' furniture came into being. One could order anything – from chests of drawers to four-poster beds – that folded and hinged for ease of transportation in the field.

Today, the most covetable antique trunks are those which survived the golden age of travel (the years prior to the Great Depression) and particularly those designed by Louis Vuitton, which can fetch up to tens of thousands at auction. Très chic firm Asprey may have been given the Royal Warrant, but the French fashion house made its name by creating flat-bottomed trunks from lightweight, airtight trianon canvas, covered in the distinctive LV logo, which could be stacked easily for long voyages. Just as today, Louis Vuitton's clever creations were sought by the wealthy and much copied by designers of the era ... some things will never change.

THE CRAFTY MINX AT HOME

Terrific *terrariums*

Terrariums are wonderful mini-ecosystems children can enjoy, no matter how small or non-existent your home garden is, or how inclement the weather outside. I like the playful element of creating a prehistoric dinosaur terrain, animal farm or bunny meadow, depending on your child's preference. Or a fairy garden full of hidden, tiny treasures and wild undergrowth set to spark the imagination.

If staying in is the new going out, this is country life for even the most urban(e) city kid.

MATERIALS NEEDED

- A lovely glass jam jar, bell jar and base, or glass vessel, such as the one pictured overleaf
- Plastic animals
- Pebbles or stones from the garden, for drainage
- Charcoal, for keeping the soil sweet
- Peat moss potting mixture, for soil and water retention
- A layer of green moss from the garden or a nursery

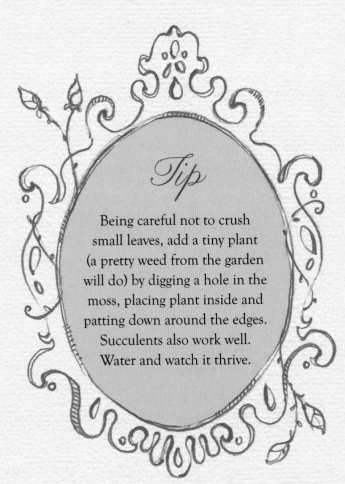

Tip

Being careful not to crush small leaves, add a tiny plant (a pretty weed from the garden will do) by digging a hole in the moss, placing plant inside and patting down around the edges. Succulents also work well. Water and watch it thrive.

PIERRE LAPIN
LA FAMILLE FLOPSAUT
TALE OF JEMIMA PUDDLE·DUCK
THE FLOPSY BUNNIES   WARNE

INSTRUCTIONS

1 Have your helper place a layer of pebbles at the bottom of your vessel before covering with a 0.5–1cm (¼–³⁄₈ in) layer of charcoal.

2 Cover charcoal with a 2–3cm (¾–1¼ in) layer of peat moss.

3 Cover peat moss with green moss and pat down into place, smoothing the edges over the other layers and curving down the sides of glass.

4 Water the moss with a half-glass of water or less, depending on the size of your vessel and how dry the moss is to begin with. That's it – your terrarium's ready to set up now with the plastic animals of your choice. Add a pebble or two for interesting natural terrain.

THE CHILD'S ROOM

Sometimes more is more (and less is a bore)

Princess & the Pea bedding

I'm a sucker for vintage paisley eiderdowns and crocheted rugs heaped upon a child's bed, which look so Dreamy English Cottage. Bright, colourful bedding sets the stage for fantasy, and an imagination free from cartoon franchise branding. Think of the biblio version of *Peter Pan*, Enid Blyton's *Magic Faraway Tree* and the old *Princess and the Pea* fairytale while tucking one's wee darlings in for the night.

Be adventurous while hunting for children's bedding in flea markets and charity stores. Just think 'more is more' (and less is a bore). Even in summer, bright folded blankets look grand atop a simple wardrobe, or stacked high upon open shelving.

Vintage eiderdowns in faded paisleys are vintage gold dust, but every once in a while, it's possible to bag a bargain. Be advised to snap them up quick smart. These can be re-feathered for a hefty price, but my advice is to give them a good handwash in the bath with a gentle wool wash and fabric softener, then leave them outside to dry in hot sunshine for a few consecutive days (best attempted in high summer). Or pop them in a large, top-loading washing machine on a delicate setting. Repair any holes or cover stains first with cleverly applied areas of appliqué and patchwork, and embroider your child's name across one corner for decoration.

Crocheted rugs are far easier to come by. Collect from eBay, charity stores and flea markets, but opt for wool or wool-mix, rather than acrylic. Many will be damaged, but I tend to repair with areas of crochet mimicking the stitches used in the rest of the blanket. For really large holes, repair with an area of contrasting crochet or wool fabric, and add decoration, such as a crocheted flower, buttons or sequinned insects, to the centre. Magical!

Strike a match

WINING AND DINING

*W*ho would you invite to your dream dinner party, given half the chance? Along with a host of treasured friends and disregarding reality, my guest list ranges wildly, from dead authors and monarchs to performers, celebrity chefs, a psychoanalyst and a fabulous nobody or two, plus a few favourite characters from novels thrown into the mix (*Nice to make your acquaintance, Miss Flora Poste*). Even if it's not a success, at the very least I've hit upon the formula for an unforgettable evening.

Much like the Georgians did, I have a fierce penchant for dinner parties and have been putting them on since the days of my hapless teenage years, if not quite as successfully. From disastrous adventures in Mexican cuisine (microwaved cheese nachos, anyone? Thought not) to the four-or-more-course adventures my husband and I spend a week planning towards, raiding our large collection of cookbooks for inspiration and traversing the city many times over in search of the best ingredients, hoping to delight and surprise our guests – I do love a chance to entertain. Because for me, dinner parties are the stuff of life. Where better to celebrate friendship, love and the passage of time than over a gastronomic feast? Even a quiet meal amongst friends is an event: I don't think there is a more persuasive way to honour the people you care about than with a generous, well-thought-out meal and the dedication of time.

If you're fortunate enough to possess a separate dining room, consider indulging in the sorts of bold decorative touches you wouldn't faintly contemplate elsewhere. Layers and layers of vintage pieces sing here, and whisper elegance with the simple addition of a crisp white tablecloth and napkins. If you want to make a lasting impression, nothing says lavish quite like gilt and candlelight reflected in mirrors *ad infinitum*. This is what crystal goblets were invented for. Burgundy paint and flock wallpaper also never looked so good. Accompany meals with dramatic lighting and a delectably set table, stimulating dinner party conversation with adventurous choices in art, sculptural table centres or taxidermy, and an impressive display of rich blooms.

Take inspiration from the French court, if you will. Even without the riches of Versailles at your disposal, why not ask yourself: what would Marie Antoinette do?

Nouveau chic table runner

Lend an air of drama to any dinner party with a bold runner placed at the heart of your table display. Paired with a well-soused collection of guests, this mauve zebra print by Florence Broadhurst reeks of '70s hedonism and the luxe life. Add Moroccan cuisine and buckets of Champagne for proper authenticity.

Find your own fab fabric version for a sensational dinner party experience. And don't forget: two Panadol and a pint of water before bed (although Mick and Bianca wouldn't have bothered).

MATERIALS NEEDED

- Heavyweight fabric, such as this gorgeous upholstery remnant
- Sewing machine and thread
- Needle
- Pearl embroidery thread and metallic thread, for tassels

INSTRUCTIONS

1. This is one easy-peasy, lemon-squeezie project – simply measure the size of table runner you want. Mine measures 40 x 100cm (16 x 39½in), because the size best features a few repeats of its fabulous zebra print.

2. Fold under the raw edge on one side, then fold it under again and straight stitch on your sewing machine to create a double hem.

3. When you come to the end of one side, snip off any excess fabric at the corner before turning and rolling under.

4. Sew along adjacent side and keep going until done.

5. To make simple tassels, wind pearl thread around three of your fingers till you have the right amount for a tassel, then carefully slip the loops from your fingers and thread a piece of matching thread through the top of all the loops and knot it, to secure them together. (Don't trim these threads, as you will use them to sew the tassel to the runner.) Take some metallic thread and wind it around the loops, a little way down from your secured end. This makes the 'neck' of the tassel – when you've wound enough, thread the end down behind the wound thread, with a needle, to stop it unravelling. Now cut and trim the loops at the bottom end and you're done (except that now you need to make another three to match).

6. Use the tying thread to stitch your tassels firmly to all four corners of your runner.

FIT FOR A FEAST

The Ancient Egyptians were quite used to civilised feasts. We know because several dining tables were found in King Tutankhamun's tomb when it was first opened back in 1922. But the table as we know it has been around in one form or another since mediaeval times, when an audience with a feudal lord would be granted at the 'high' table and everybody else would make do with the floor.

As with everything else, the dining table was seen as a symbol of social power, wealth and status and, with this in mind, developed from a simple plank of timber and iron nail construction to such wonderful examples as the 16th century Florentine coloured travertine marble dining tables. Given the sturdiness of the materials used, these have largely survived in good working order and provide a magnificent insight into the design and craftsmanship of the era. Florentine tables boast a decorative inlaid top on a cast-iron base, and were

DINING
TABLES
OF YORE

THE CRAFTY MINX AT HOME

created around the time Da Vinci was painting The Last Supper. But whereas his was quite a simple Milanese refectory table, and probably constructed from walnut or some such timber, Florentine examples were exquisite works of art. With patrons such as the Famiglia d' Medici (or the House of Medici, a political dynasty, banking family and later royal house) commissioning them, it is little wonder; each piece of stone was hand carved to the exact shape required, and painstakingly fitted together. The distinctive tables still command high prices in salerooms across the world to this day.

Other wonderful examples of grand dining effects are to be seen in the Georgian period, or 18th to early 19th centuries. Craftsmanship of the era was outstanding, with exquisite mahogany extension dining tables boasting clever winding mechanisms and pedestal bases, which meant that each component could fit together neatly or be used as a table in its own right (and so the legs wouldn't get in the way). Rich mahogany from Cuba or Honduras was beautifully cut to show off its flame effect, with edges inlaid with lighter wood details, using box or satinwood. Legs were often carved with exotic animalia (think lion's paws) and design generally followed the style of the day.

The Georgians were big fans of symmetry and, often, the sideboards or chiffoniers, placed near the dining table to serve, were architectural in form, or at least made with a nod to the building styles of the day. These included column or half-column pilasters, uprights flanking doors with arches, or backboards with pediment features. To add the finishing touches to the whole Greco/Roman, awe-inspiring effect, the Georgians' use of wall sconces resembling torches, plant stands, cellarettes in the shape of sarcophagi, and the finest silverware and crystal money could buy made fine dining an experience like none other.

L'air du temps
table sculpture

It was the textile designer and artist William Morris who first advised: 'Have nothing in your houses that you do not know to be useful, or believe to be beautiful', a quote which formed the basis for the highly popular Arts and Crafts movement of 19th-century England. Bell jars are both. Originally designed for scientific use and to create a vacuum for the preservation of butterflies and taxidermy, they are now a highly collectable form of industrial design in their own right, providing a wonderful way to display all manner of objets in a quirky, modern way.

My bell jars play host to an oft-changing collection of ceramics, crocheted curiosities and found objects, such as feathers, dried flowers or seed pods. Create your own striking table centre under a bell jar dome, and theme its display to complement the mood you're trying to create. This one here sets the stage for a Bollywood-themed Indian feast; simply lay the table with a brightly hued Indian sari.

MATERIALS NEEDED

- Glass dome
- Base to match
- Reclaimed found objects, such as broken toys, jewellery, leaves and bones
- Additional decorative items, such as beads, feathers and sequins
- Craft glue
- Paint
- Thin wire and wire cutters

Bell jars provide a wonderful way to display all manner of objects in a quirky, modern way

INSTRUCTIONS

1. Here, I've decided to decorate a ceramic pheasant with neon pompoms, jewellery, beads and feathers, to use as my table centre sculpture. Find your own feathered friend or discarded toy, and start experimenting in a similar way.

2. Affix decorative items with glue and add paint if needed, allowing your sculpture to dry completely.

3. Take your wire and carefully insert into your creation's underside. Many old bell jars have a central depression or hole for items to be carefully displayed in an upright position, but you might need to create one to poke the wire into, if you're worried your item won't stay standing.

4. Array other found objects on the base, cover with a clean polished dome, and place in the centre of your table for maximum effect. Choose any item which is small, quirky and fits with your colour theme. The only limit, as always, is your imagination

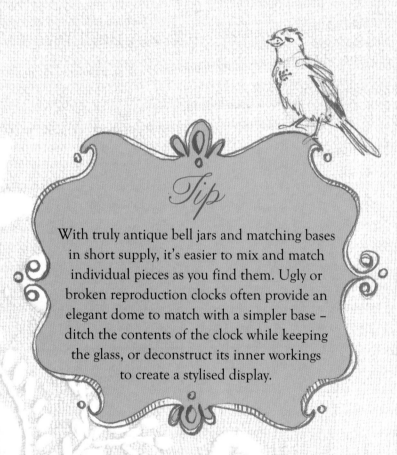

Tip

With truly antique bell jars and matching bases in short supply, it's easier to mix and match individual pieces as you find them. Ugly or broken reproduction clocks often provide an elegant dome to match with a simpler base – ditch the contents of the clock while keeping the glass, or deconstruct its inner workings to create a stylised display.

THE CRAFTY MINX AT HOME

THE GOOD SILVER

DAZZLING
DINING
PARAPHERNALIA

Exquisite cutlery, which peaked in the 18th and 19th centuries, needed an equally fabulous box to house it, as silver cutlery was, by its very nature of being part of a set, prone to loss over the years. It's not entirely clear how the term 'Canteen of Cutlery' arose, but it's thought to have come from an Italian or French household or even military usage, and most people who own silverware today will find a partial Canteen or item of cutlery in a pattern they like, and spend a lifetime matching it up as near to the original as possible. This is a nice way to build a collection, and can be an inexpensive (if lengthy) process. To find a complete set with identical hallmarks (that is, by the same maker in the same year of manufacture and assayed at the same office) is virtually impossible and, as with most things, the best examples are housed in private collections in the stately homes of Europe or can be found in public museums.

The dining experience would not be considered complete without drinking glasses and decanters. Glass comes in various degrees of quality and is made with the addition of lead. When comparing colourless glass, there is a variant from yellow to grey (depending on the lead content), and the sound of well-cut crystal when pinged with a fingernail is music to a connoisseur's ears. Early decoration included adding air and twisting the glass when blowing, as well as faceting or cutting flat facets on the stem and engraving the bowl. By Victorian times, the use of coloured glass and gilding was widespread, and techniques for glass production became highly sophisticated – particularly in Europe, with centres, such as Bohemia and Murano, seen as meccas for trade still to this day. Despite all the clever techniques and jewel-like quality of expensive crystal, there is something timeless and understated in the early drinking glasses, which often have slight faults and inclusions, as they were all hand-blown. But these are becoming scarcer to find and are highly collectable.

201

Convert discarded books into a thing of beauty

Fleeting beauty
paper florals

The repurposing of discarded books in paper art has become very popular over the past decade or so. Many consider it sacrilege to destroy a book, but there are so many damaged and unwanted tomes just languishing in charity stores or on bookshelves, it seems as good a use as any to convert them to something of beauty.

Using paper printed with words or imagery, these faux flowers can look even better than the real thing, and provide a delicate and unusual decorative effect for any table. Make a stack of them for a special occasion. Children will love to get in on the act, also, so ask for their help and set up a mini production line.

MATERIALS NEEDED

- A book – hunt for ruined, unwanted tomes at your local charity store
- Craft knife
- Plain brown paper, recycled from a bag or from a roll
- A glass
- Pencil
- Paper scissors
- Skewer
- Split pin brads, from stationery or scrapbooking supplies stores

INSTRUCTIONS

1. Detach pages from the book by breaking apart the book's spine, or use a craft knife to remove.

2. Using the glass rim as a template, trace the pencil around its circumference and cut out.

3. Repeat until you have 6–8 circles.

4. Cut leaf shapes from the brown paper, large enough to be seen around the edges of the circles.

5. Skewer holes in the centre of each circle and one end of each leaf.

6. Take your brad and work it gently through each of the holes until all layers are secured, adding the leaves last. Fold the split pins apart underneath.

7. Crinkle up the edges of the paper circles, one after the other, starting with the one in the middle. Use your scissors to nick small, triangular-shaped pieces randomly from the edges to create a more realistic petal shape.

8. Repeat the above steps until you have enough for your display, and arrange down the centre of the dining table.

THE CRAFTY MINX AT HOME

I love the nightlife
lampshade

Some people excel at throwing debauched parties. I'm not one of them, I'm afraid, although most dinner parties at our house tend to conclude with a lively dancing session in the kitchen, everyone in their cups, and stereo elevated to a volume the neighbours most likely do not appreciate. Playing rock songs more than this well-known disco tune, but the sentiment's still the same. (Early Kings of Leon, anyone? I'm partial to a spot of 'Taper Jean Girl' myself. Or the Rolling Stones' 'Sympathy for the Devil').

Even something as simple as a new lampshade can really change a room overall and inject a sense of revelry, especially over the dining table. Seek out ugly but well-sized shades from flea markets or charity stores, and cover them with a new length of fabric in a glamorous makeover. Many op-shop frames are still worth saving, with any dust and discolouration easily hidden underneath a new layer of skin. This is a great way to show off vintage upholstery fabrics and less wearable materials you may have picked up on your perambulations.

MATERIALS NEEDED

- Recycled drum lampshade
- Butcher's paper
- Pencil
- Dressmaker's and paper scissors
- Reclaimed or new fabric – upholstery-weight linen will be better than light cotton for this purpose
- Iron
- Spray adhesive
- Ruler

INSTRUCTIONS

1. Take your lampshade and place upon the butcher's paper, with the seam touching the left edge of the paper.

2. Roll shade to the right, drawing a line on the paper along the top edge of the shade as you go.

3. When you reach the seam again on the far right side of the paper, draw a line down the seam edge of the lampshade, adding an extra 2.5cm (1in) at the end for it to overlap.

4. Roll the shade back to the left, drawing along the bottom edge until you have a curved or rectangular-looking block. This will be your pattern.

5. Cut out the shape drawn on the paper and place on the wrong side of the fabric, using it as a pattern to cut out the fabric needed to cover your lampshade.

6. Fold over 1cm (3/8 in) on one straight edge of the fabric, where the seams should meet and iron flat.

7. Turn over the fabric so it's facing right side down, and cover the wrong side evenly with a thin layer of spray adhesive.

8. Holding the adhesive-covered fabric carefully with your fingertips, place the raw seam edge along the initial seam, and slowly pat down into place. Roll the fabric over the entire surface of the lampshade, making sure to smooth any bubbles that might be forming as you go. You may need to use the ruler to help flatten any bubbles between the two layers.

9. When you reach the adjoining seam, pat the iron-folded edge down into place and allow to dry.

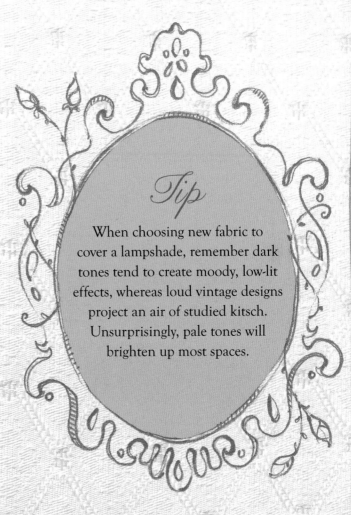

Tip

When choosing new fabric to cover a lampshade, remember dark tones tend to create moody, low-lit effects, whereas loud vintage designs project an air of studied kitsch. Unsurprisingly, pale tones will brighten up most spaces.

Boom goes my beating heart

KITCHENS WITH SOUL

Of all the kitchens I've known, my favourite is the messy, poky heart of a former boyfriend's family home, located on the ground floor of his bursting-at-the-seams terrace and overlooking a sprawling garden and ramshackle shed. With three brothers, lovely parents and a handful of friends, pets and misfits (that would be me) arranged around the kitchen's farmhouse table and pews, sharing a meal in the Shaker-style environs, it remains in my memory as one of the most comforting and welcoming spaces I knew for a time. Or the eggshell-enamelled, Aga-dominated room of my dear friend Katie's family pile in rural Gloucestershire, preferably with her, propped atop the ancient stove to warm her behind. Neither are particularly modern or stylish kitchens, but both positively pulsate with the love of a thousand shared family meals and experiences, conveying the notion of everything a kitchen should be about.

Over the course of a single day, we visit the kitchen perhaps more than any other room in the home. It's a place where functionality and cleanliness are important, but warmth and charm also play such an important part in making this core area more inviting and nourishing. Aim for more than just gleaming white or metal surfaces concealing every last implement, plate or scrap of personality from view. Wear your heart on your sleeve by displaying favoured collections, family photographs and artworks or reclaimed pieces that reveal something about you. The sort of kitsch indulgences we give short shrift to elsewhere, for example, are somehow appropriate in the place where we make endless pots of tea, listen to the radio,

gather with friends or family to prepare three meals a day and share what we've been up to, in an informal setting.

Kitchens and bathrooms – being prime centres of utility as well as indulgence – tend to date and become tired more quickly than other rooms of the home. Work with what you've got to update over time, if you can, rather than in one fell swoop. The very best homes seem to do this, accumulating character in meaningful layers, rather than throwing the metaphorical baby out with the bathwater in favour of stark modern practicality.

If you do need to update fixtures and fittings, carefully plan your layout and really think about where everything needs to go. Create a floor plan to scale, and practise moving about in it for guidance on what works and what doesn't. Look to recycled wooden doors or signage to elevate from the mundane, and judge whether a current item can be reinvented with simple sanding and a new paintjob. Open shelving is more challenging to fill in a visually appealing way, but can look really quirky and wonderful with the right ingredients – decorated with a useful stack of vintage tea towels, say, or flea market bowls and jugs of every description. Make every little nook count by displaying its own virtual still life, which looks intriguing and is possible to carry off in even the most frequented corners of the kitchen.

I love this aesthetic, which takes into account an appreciation for the old and the new, feels completely authentic, and is ultimately a gloriously unique expression of character.

Cute curator kitchen curtains

Anyone with an older-style kitchen will be familiar with the quandary of open cupboards. Yes, they're lovely for displaying the more attractive items in your cooking arsenal, but what of the functional (and ugly) metal utensils, pots, pans and Pyrex bowls you simply can't live without? Cover 'em up, I say, with a pretty and unique patchworked curtain. And why not create a window treatment to match, while you're at it?

This is possibly the simplest and most effective use of all those scraps of vintage fabric, reclaimed cross-stitch, solo damask napkins and beautiful old threads you'll ever find, but are loathe to actually use. You won't regret finally putting them to use but, if you do, a quick unpick will restore them to their original state.

After all the gleaming surfaces of Nineties and Noughties minimalism, isn't it nice to have a more personal kitchen? Why, hello there, Miss Suzy Homemaker.

MATERIALS NEEDED

- Various scraps of vintage fabric, cross-stitching, hankies and anything else you fancy the look of, fabric-wise
- Measuring tape
- Sewing machine or needle and thread
- Dressmaker's scissors
- Curtain rod and hooks

212

*A pretty use for doilies and
old scraps of vintage fabric*

INSTRUCTIONS

1. Simply measure the width of the cupboard you plan to cover, and add an extra third to this measurement, if you'd like the curtain to ruche prettily. Measure and make a note of the height as well.

2. Attach your curtain rod hooks to the cupboard internally, one on either side. Hardware stores and places like IKEA stock some excellent, easy-to-install versions that don't even need screwing into place and work with springs and plastic hook doodads.

3. Start laying out your fabric, playing with the effect of combining smaller and larger pieces together until the overall look is *just so*. Be aware that you'll lose between 1–2cm ($^3/_8$–$^3/_4$ in) from the width and height of each piece when you sew them all together, and will need another few centimetres at the top to cover the curtain rod.

4. When you're happy with how it's all looking, start sewing the pieces together with a tacking stitch for a less permanent fix, or small stitches on the machine if making to last.

5. After it's completed, trim the edges to the correct size, and hem along the bottom and both sides by pressing under 0.5cm ($^1/_4$ in), then another 0.5cm ($^1/_4$ in) for a double hem and sewing into place, to avoid fraying.

6. Fold enough fabric over at the top to cover your curtain rod, tucking under the raw edges as well and sewing in a straight line across.

7. Slide onto your rod and settle into place, Miss Curator of lovely things.

CANNY KITCHEN STORAGE: DRESSOIRS

Storage in the modern home has always been a bit of a battle between chic versus utility. The current trend for storing away household paraphernalia behind vast gleaming laminate configurations (particularly in the kitchen) can look impressive, but feel somewhat soulless. On the other hand, the kitchen which favours standalone pieces can look cramped or contain little necessary shelving and cupboard space if it is put together without flair and careful consideration.

The kitchen dresser, often known as a buffet or hutch, is one of the most useful pieces of furniture one can own. The word 'dresser' itself comes from the mediaeval French *dressoir*, which was originally more of a table or plank on legs set against a wall, with shelves placed above or nearby, where one would literally dress and prepare the food. In time, the various components became assembled and through the ages, craftsmen embellished them with all manner of decoration such as dates, initials, flora and fauna, emblems, etcetera.

214

If you have beautiful porcelain china, why hide it away? The traditional kitchen dresser has built-in plate racks or contains a strip of timber along the edge of its shelves to attractively display plates and prevent them from toppling. There is usually a carved overhang as well, with the whole thing resting upon on a solid cupboard base (containing more useful shelves below a set of drawers). Yet more styles are raised on legs, with a pot board or stretcher base.

Kitchen dressers come in all shapes and sizes, but the most loved is probably the Welsh dresser, made from oak or pine and dating back to the late 17th or early 18th centuries. Although the term Welsh dresser implies Welsh origin, these were actually made throughout the surrounding counties, and with regional variations in style. Many a manner of timber and adornment evolved, with European fruitwood examples boasting beautiful iron or brass escutcheons and handles, and in Northern Europe, in particular, they became heavily carved, usually with game hunting scenes.

Up until modern times, the dresser traditionally formed part of a young woman's dowry when entering into marriage, which also makes it quite a romantic piece of furniture, when you think about it. Passed down from generation to generation, dressers spoke of a family's hopes for their daughter's future, and became scarred over time with various dints and nicks from use. This has made the more rustic pieces even more beautiful and collectible for modern buyers, and antique examples still fetch excellent prices at auction today.

Happy days
vintage tea towel napkins

There was a time when many household rituals revolved around the taking of tea, and the beverage beloved of England and its colonies was consumed morning, noon and night. Between the wars and in times of austerity, dinner parties may have been seldom thrown affairs, but the tea party took centre stage in the social activities of most families and towns, providing a much-anticipated opportunity for women to congregate together and share gossip while the children played or were expected to quietly partake. The hostess would wear a natty dress, heels, stocking and corset – even though her frock would traditionally be covered with a frilly apron – and arrange hair, makeup and progeny just so in readiness for the big event.

In the spirit of kitchen kitsch, make these tea towel napkins to accompany refreshments at an afternoon tea party, picking out favourite imagery with embroidered sections. Take your cue from cluelessly batty Mrs Cunningham, from television's *Happy Days*, when applying a wholesome quote or two, or provoke commentary with some Tracey Emin-inspired subversion, emblazoning cheeky messages or slogans across their fronts in backstitch – take your pick.

MATERIALS NEEDED

- A selection of vintage tea towels
- Ruler
- Dressmaker's chalk
- Dressmaker's scissors
- Sewing machine and thread
- Pearl embroidery threads in different colours
- Embroidery needle

INSTRUCTIONS

1. Lay out your selection of favourite vintage tea towels and decide upon the best square of fabric to cut from each – each napkin will require a finished square measuring about 40 x 40cm (16 x 16in) – so be sure to leave some hem allowance. I've simply cut mine in half.

2. Press under and sew a narrow double hem around all four edges. Use an embroidery stitch (such as satin stitch or running stitch) to pick out favoured motifs in one corner of each napkin, so that when it is folded the needlework will be visible for guests to see.

3. To stitch on a written message, use your dressmaker's pencil to write the words or phrase, and stitch over the lines with a backstitch.

4. Create at least four of these napkins – 10 should be enough to impress a large party of guests with your handiwork.

Gracious host
sweetheart apron

J'adore a vintage half-apron, particularly the lovingly hand-stitched or embellished kind, created with a good dash of wit and taste by owners past. Often made to be worn as accessories to every housewifely get-up, shortie aprons have been steadily replaced by the fuller and more utilitarian styles over the years, which are worn less but expected to work harder to protect our clothes.

I own a small collection of flirty handmade half-aprons, but have little cause to wear them – apart from serving up tea to friends in a nostalgic nod to the high tea style of yesteryear.

Add a sweetheart bib to a vintage half-apron, and wear as a sort of half-dress while cooking or serving. Even flung over jeans and T-shirt they look grand, but even better frocked-out with heels and a slick of red lipstick. You'll feel oh-so-fabulous pulling those freshly baked tarts out of the oven, you Domestic Goddess you.

MATERIALS NEEDED

- Vintage half-apron
- Matching or contrasting fabric for bib, approximately 40 x 40cm (16 x 16in)
- Woven cotton tape or remnant fabric, for halter-neck strap
- Bias binding
- Iron
- Vintage lace
- Dressmaker's scissors
- Sewing machine and thread
- Needle

INSTRUCTIONS

1. Find a worthy fabric partner for your pretty apron in a haberdashery, or salvage a complementary piece from another vintage find – don't forget to compare both to see which designs work well together, as some might delight and others clash disharmoniously when bought separately.

2. Pop on your apron and hold the square of bib fabric up against yourself to see how it fits.

3. Cut a loose heart shape with a wider base and pin to the existing apron until it looks a perfect fit against your figure.

4. Stitch bias binding around edges of bib by sewing first one edge of binding to the wrong side, then folding it over, ironing flat and stitching remaining edge at the front.

5. To create a fabric halter-neck strap like the one used here, fold over a long strip of fabric, right sides together, and sew along the raw edges to create a tube.

6. Turn right side out, iron flat, and fold short raw edges under. (These will be secured in place when you attach the straps.)

7. Attach your cotton tape or fabric halter-neck strap to each side of the bib's top with pins and stitch, reversing a few times at either side for strength.

8. Attach bib to apron with a line of stitching, then hand-stitch lace over your machine stitching. Why hello – are you being served?

OR MAKE YOUR OWN EASY VINTAGE-STYLE APRON ...

MATERIALS NEEDED

- 80 x 40cm (31¼ x 16in) soft cotton in a pretty pattern (vintage '50s is ideal, so look for old tablecloths or damaged dresses from this era to cut up if you can't find the right fabric in a bolt)
- 150 x 10cm (59 x 4in) plain fabric in a contrasting colour
- Measuring tape
- 25mm- (1in-) wide bias binding to match plain fabric
- Dressmaker's scissors
- Sewing machine and thread
- Iron

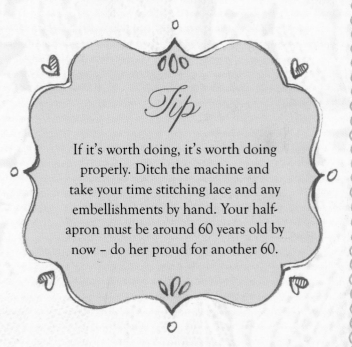

Tip

If it's worth doing, it's worth doing properly. Ditch the machine and take your time stitching lace and any embellishments by hand. Your half-apron must be around 60 years old by now – do her proud for another 60.

INSTRUCTIONS

1 Fold your fabric in half crosswise so it measures 40 x 40cm (16 x 16in). Using a dinner plate or something similar, trace a curve onto the outer bottom corner of the double fabric and cut along your traced line, through both layers, to create rounded edges on the bottom of your apron skirt. Open out the rectangle again.

2 Press the bias binding in half along its length, wrong sides together. Slip the raw edge of the apron skirt between the folded edges of the binding and use your machine to stitch the bias binding around the sides and bottom of the rectangle, taking care to ease it around the curved bottom edges.

3 Measure along the top raw edge of the apron and mark the centre point with a pin. Starting at this centre point, make a number of evenly spaced 1–2cm (³⁄₈–³⁄₄in) pleats across the top of the apron towards the side edge in one direction, then return to the centre point and make the same number of pleats towards the side edge in the other direction. Hold each pleat in place with a pin. When you have finished, your apron should measure about 40–44cm (16–17¹⁄₂in) across the top edge – if it doesn't, adjust some of your pleats on each side of the centre point until it does.

4 Now stitch across the top edge, about 5mm (¹⁄₄in) down from the raw edge, to hold all the pleats in position, removing the pins as you sew.

5 Fold your plain fabric waistband strip in half crosswise and mark the centre point of one long edge with a pin. Open out again.

6 With right sides together and raw edges even, pin the pleated apron to the marked long edge of the waistband strip, matching the marked centre points. Allowing a 1cm (³⁄₈in) seam, stitch the apron to the waistband as pinned.

7 Pull the skirt of the apron down over the seam and press it with your iron.

8 Now fold the waistband strip in half lengthwise on itself, bringing right sides together.

9 Use your ruler and scissors to trim both short ends of the folded waistband at an angle – this isn't absolutely necessary, but it looks pretty when finished.

10 Allowing a 1cm (³⁄₈in) seam, stitch across one short end of the waistband, pivot on the needle at the corner and stitch along the lower raw edges until you get to the edge of the skirt. Reverse-stitch a little to stop the seam unravelling. Repeat this process for the other end of the waistband.

11 Turn the waistband right side out, pushing out the angled corners with your fingers.

12 Turn under the remaining raw edge on the waistband and pin in place. Now stitch right around the edge of the waistband, stitching close to all four edges. This closes the remaining part of the seam and gives a nice top-stitched finish.

If it's worth doing, it's worth doing properly

222

Coming up roses
serving tray

It's easy to consider most decoupage projects a mammoth undertaking, consisting of many days of work, sanding, cutting, pasting, applying lacquer and patience in allowing drying time – and indeed it is on larger projects. But the skill works equally well on smaller items, such as trays and bedside table surfaces, and takes very little time in reality, when kept nearby for quick coats of lacquer. These are easy to apply in quiet moments between other activities.

I'd owned this bamboo tea platter for many years, but it was starting to look tired, with its chipped paint and stains from too many overflowing pots of Russian Caravan. I painted it a rosy pink, added a handful of paper blooms chopped from an otherwise trashed book of Redouté's Roses, and a Marie Antoinette-inspired postcard from Versailles that my friend Katrina gave me, in the centre. All in all, it took less than a couple of hours to complete and I'm thrilled with the outcome, extending the life of my tray for many years to come and allowing me to serve tea *sans* a pretty tea towel underneath in future.

Tip

You can buy readymade decoupage glue from craft stores, but a less expensive option is to mix three parts white PVA glue, such as Aquadhere, with one part water. Good old Clag school paste can also be used, although it's better to strengthen it a little with one part PVA to three parts Clag. If you're using very delicate paper cutouts, it's also better to find a rubber roller to remove air bubbles, rather than risk tearing your work with a ruler.

MATERIALS NEEDED

- A wooden serving tray or platter
- Paper for decoupage
- Small, sharp scissors
- Sandpaper and block
- Cloth
- Paint
- Paintbrush
- Digital camera
- Decoupage glue
- Ruler or rubber roller
- Lacquer

INSTRUCTIONS

1 Chop up your paper pieces and arrange them over the platter in a pleasing formation. Use your digital camera to snap a quick image, just to remind you where each piece should go when you're ready to apply glue.

2 Prepare the wood by lightly sanding its surface, and use a damp cloth to remove any dust until it is clean and smooth.

3 Paint over the surface with two to three coats of acrylic paint, allowing the correct drying time stated on the tin between coats.

4 Apply decoupage glue to the surface of the tray and position your paper pieces on the glue. Gently brush more glue over the surface of the pieces and work any air bubbles to the edges. When you've applied each layer, use a rubber roller or ruler to gently apply pressure and skim the surface of the paper, squeezing bubbles and glue out from between the paper and the tray. Wipe away any excess glue with a damp cloth.

5 Allow to dry for at least 24 hours.

6 Once you're happy with the paper arrangement and it's all completely dry, apply a coat of lacquer with your brush using small, careful strokes. Allow to dry.

7 Apply a further two coats, allowing ample drying time in between. You're ready to roll.

The heirloom collection

Granny would be proud, lady – especially now her intact 80-piece tea set's been broken up or scattered to the four winds by previous generations. Make your own everyday trio from a combination of the finest single articles you can find, for pure girly indulgence at elevenses. Mix and match for chic perfection, and create your own personal cache of china for decadent high teas with a bevy of your favourite women.

Try sticking to a theme, such as roses, birds, gilt or pastels, and refine your ultimate heirloom collection as you add each piece.

For a completely useful set, seek to find the following pieces:

- One fabulous teapot
- A bowl or ceramic pot with lid, for serving sugar cubes
- One or two milk jugs
- 8–10 single teacups
- 8–10 saucers
- 8–10 small plates
- One tiered cake display for macarons, cupcakes and the like
- A large decorative plate or two for larger cakes and tarts
- Top off the collection with a random selection of vintage souvenir teaspoons, and you're done. Lovely.

Hello, is it tea you're looking for?
tea cosies

We might be a breezy bunch, we Australians, but we do love an excuse for frocking up and sharing High Tea. Our European communities formed a nation of coffee lovers, but I wonder whether the tide might be turning in favour of the refined charms of tea drinking, and our English settler roots?

The humble tea cosy went the way of the dodo over the past few decades, but has returned with a passion. One need only look to the bestselling success of inspired knitter Loani Prior's *Wild Tea Cosy* books for evidence of this. A tea cosy parading as a tropical coral reef, anyone?

These are two whimsies whipped up in an hour or two. Spend your time compiling favourite scraps and woolly bits, and the rest almost takes care of itself.

THE CRAFTY MINX *AT HOME*

*Coffee's great, but I prefer
the refined ritual of tea drinking*

MATERIALS NEEDED FOR FABRIC TEA COSY

- 4 half-ovals of linen, enough to fit over your favourite teapot and then some for the seam allowance – mine was made from remnant scraps, found in an upholsterer's clearance bin
- Thin strip of Liberty Tana lawn, for top loop and bottom edge
- Prettily printed fabric for appliqué – look to animals, flowers and birds, or abstract designs shaped to resemble clouds and trees
- Dressmaker's scissors
- Small amount wool/polyester filling
- Starry sequins
- Needle
- Metallic gold thread
- Pearl embroidery thread
- Thin quilt batting
- Sewing machine and thread
- Iron

INSTRUCTIONS

1 Cut two strips of Liberty print to fit along the lower edges of two half-ovals (front and back of cosy). Press under the raw edge along one long edge of each strip. Aligning the raw edges at the sides and bottom, topstitch the strips in place along the straight bottom edge of your ovals. (You only need to stitch along the pressed edge of the strip, but if you stitch around the raw edges too, it keeps everything in place until you sew the seam.)

2 Appliqué printed animals, birds or other shapes to each outer half-oval, poking in a small amount of filling before completing stitching, to provide a little puff.

3 Hand-quilt with metallic thread, and get creative with your sequins, beads or buttons for decoration.

4 Cut two pieces of thin batting to the same size as your remaining undecorated half-ovals (lining).

5 Pin the batting shapes to the wrong side of each lining half-oval and stitch in place around the outer edge, about 1cm ($^3/_8$ in) from the edge. To reduce bulk, trim away the excess seam allowance from the batting only, cutting as close as possible to the stitching.

6 With right sides together, stitch the lining sections to the outer sections along the lower straight edge.

7 Create a loop by folding a strip of Liberty print in half lengthwise, right sides together, stitching along the long raw edge and turning inside out. Iron flat.

8 With right sides facing each other, place the cosy sections together, lining against lining, outer section against outer section, and straight seams aligned. Slip the loop between the outer layers at the top, with raw edges poking out.

9 Stitch around all edges, leaving an 8cm ($3^1/_4$ in) opening in the lining seam.

10 Turn the cosy right side out through the opening in the lining, stitch the opening closed, then push the lining inside the cosy.

MATERIALS NEEDED FOR FELT TEA COSY

- 2 half-ovals of thick felt or old shrunken jumper, enough to fit over your favourite teapot and then some for the seam allowance
- Felt pompom balls
- Needle and pearl embroidery thread

INSTRUCTIONS

1 Decorate half-ovals with hand-stitched pompoms, buttons or interesting felt shapes on one piece or both.

2 With wrong sides facing each other, stitch together by hand with needle and embroidery thread, along the curved edges, popping a fabric loop into the seam at the top as you stitch.

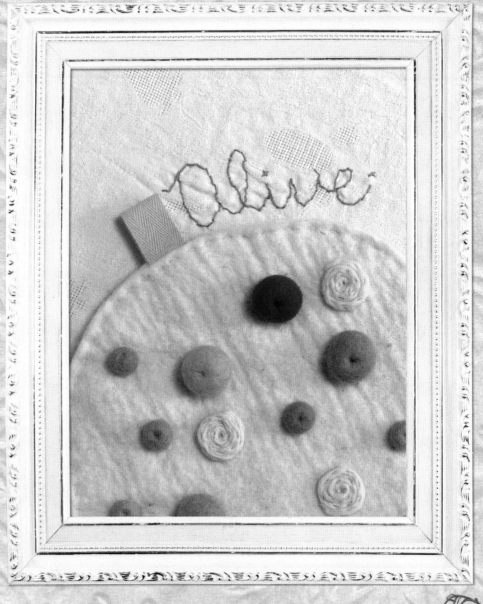

Soft landing
tie cushions

I'd rather sit on an upholstered chair than a hard wooden one but, then again, wouldn't anyone? I created these recycled rice sack tie-cushions to comfort the *derrière* while sitting at our not-very-ergonomic kitchen table, which is where I do all my writing. They work equally well for outdoor settings or any other chair in the home – the most difficult part of their construction is finding the groovy grain sacks in the first place, and matching them to your decor. First stop should be any cavernous ethnic grocery store stocking interesting wares from overseas. Try the multicultural areas of your city or town, and assiduously investigate every nook and corner for their atmospheric wares.

MATERIALS NEEDED

- Old rice or grain sacks with interesting fonts or illustrations
- 50 x 50cm (20 x 20in) cushion inserts
- 50cm (20in) zip for each cushion
- Contrasting ribbon
- Dressmaker's scissors
- Sewing machine
- Quick Unpick / seam ripper

INSTRUCTIONS

1. For large sacks, cut to size, 52 x 52cm (20½ x 20½in), and sew along sides and bottom edge, or simply trim the open hem to size.

2. Use your machine to attach the zipper to the opening, and insert your cushion.

3. Place on seat, and work out where ribbons will need to go for tie-backs (you'll need two for each back corner).

4. Unpick the seam by about 2.5cm (1in), insert ribbons and sew into place, reversing a few times for strength. Bingo – these are such a winner.

Road to bliss

SWOON-WORTHY BATHROOMS

*S*imilarly to kitchens, cleanliness and practicality take priority in the bathroom, but by no means must you leave personality at the door. Reclaimed, handcrafted and colourful pieces put to unusual purposes look really fabulous and make such a bold visual statement, especially against white. You might be surprised by how much a few small decorative touches seem to add to your pleasure in spending time there: cool, gleaming space may well be streamlined, but who wants to hang about? Some of the best bathrooms marry practical shelving and necessary items effortlessly with a humorous or luxurious element, reflecting a sense of offbeat charm or totally indulgent opulence.

If it's just you, why not go all-out plush: consider reclaimed chandeliers instead of simple light fixtures, lime-washed wooden storage crates, calming shades of hyacinth, blush or clotted cream for the walls and the best cotton bath sheets money can buy. Jewel-toned glasses to store toothbrushes or tweezers and a Venetian mirror in lieu of a simple glass pane will make you feel more pampered than Cleopatra, even without the most magnificent bathtub in the world.

For families, ample storage is key: woven baskets for toys and discarded clothing, old medicine cabinets mounted on the wall, metal lockers, a bank of pigeonholes or train luggage racks to store folded towels all maximise space while adding character. A brightly painted chair or handmade mobile also says, *enjoy.*

It's important to remember as well that none of this is forever. With the basic fittings and fixtures of a modern bathroom, all elements can be changed, based on the current mood or your family's needs.

Now lie back, sink under the steaming water, and switch off: surely one of life's finer pleasures?

Reclaimed, handcrafted and colourful pieces look fabulous in bathrooms

Aloha mama
retro organiser

Give me an inspiring pop of colour while I'm at my daily toilette, please. Everyone knows the best ideas occur while you're in the shower (at least mine do – so much so, my loved ones frequently take dictation when these ideas randomly occur, lest they be eternally forgotten).

Modern bathrooms tend to see clutter removed from all surfaces and items stored away in bland cabinets, boxes and shelves, but where's the craft in that? Tidiness is fab, but I find myself longing for a touch of personality. I created this wall organiser to break up the pure white of my bathroom walls, and display the more attractive and useful items in our toilette arsenal. If nothing else, it brightens the beginning of each day.

MATERIALS NEEDED

- Approximately 1m (40in) oilcloth fabric
- Ruler
- Pen
- Dressmaker's scissors
- Sewing machine and thread
- 25mm- (1in-) wide bias binding
- 50 x 60cm (20 x 24in) sheet of firm cardboard or 3mm ($\frac{1}{8}$in) particle board, purchased from a hardware store
- Needle
- 55cm (21$\frac{1}{2}$in) length of 20mm- ($\frac{3}{4}$in-) diameter dowel
- Ribbon

Tip

Consider those items you would like to store and display in your organiser first, and create pocket sizes accordingly to fit – that way, every loose item in your bathroom should find itself a home.

THE CRAFTY MINX AT HOME

INSTRUCTIONS

1 Lay out your oilcloth and measure and cut two rectangles, each 71 x 53cm (28 x 21in). On the wrong side of the remaining oilcloth, measure and rule up two strips, each 46cm wide x 18cm high (18¼ x 7in), and one strip 46cm wide x 13cm high (18¼ x 5in). Cut out the three strips.

2 Stitch a length of bias binding along the top edge of each of the strips, to bind the edge.

3 Take one of the oilcloth rectangles and the 13cm- (5in-) high strip. With right sides facing each other, position the strip on the rectangle, equidistant from each side edge, so that the long unbound edge is 21cm (8¼in) below the top edge and the binding is pointing towards the bottom. Allowing a 1cm (⅜in) seam, stitch the strip in place along the unbound edge, starting and finishing the seam 1cm (⅜in) in from each end.

4 Fold the strip upwards over the seam. Fold under 1cm (⅜in) on each end of the strip and topstitch the sides in place, reinforcing the stitching at the top of the seam.

5 Now repeat Steps 3 and 4 for the remaining pocket strips, positioning the lower edge of the middle strip 20cm (8in) below the bottom of the top strip, and the lower edge of the bottom strip 22cm (9in) below the bottom of the middle strip.

6 Now measure and mark the divisions on your pockets. I divided the top two pockets into three, and the bottom pocket in half – but you can customise your divisions to suit your storage needs. Topstitch the divisions in place, reinforcing the stitching at the top of the seam.

7 Lay the second oilcloth rectangle on top of the first, right sides together and raw edges matching. Allowing 1cm (⅜in) seams, stitch the sides, leaving the top and bottom edges open. Turn the organiser right side out.

8 Fold the top edges over to the back by about 4.5cm (1¾in) and stitch close to the edge through all layers, to create a casing.

9 Slip the backing board inside the oilcloth cover, fold in the lower edges and hand-sew the bottom edge closed. You're nearly done!

10 Slip the dowel into the casing. Cut a length of ribbon for a hanger and tie one end to each end of the dowel. The organiser is now ready to hang from a hook in the wall.

Keep it clean
storage cases

You can never have too many clever storage options. These useful cases look best when constructed from a range of complementary fabric designs, and work really well for storing all manner of things. You might want to make some for other areas of the home as well – smaller versions are great for keeping jewellery, keys, small change and other odds and ends in organised compartments.

MATERIALS NEEDED

- Heavy linen or upholstery fabric remnants in three different designs, including reclaimed tapestry such as this
- Ruler
- Dressmaker's scissors
- Sewing machine and thread
- Braid or decorative ribbon

*You can never have too
many clever storage options*

INSTRUCTIONS

1 These measurements will make a soft basket that is 15cm (6in) square x 18cm (7in) high. Cut two rectangles, each 38 x 17cm (15 x 6¾in), from each of two of your oilcloth designs (four rectangles in all), and two 17cm (6¾in) squares from the other design.

2 Lay out all four rectangles, side by side along the 38cm (15in) edge, alternating the designs. With right sides together and allowing 1cm (⅜in) seams, sew the rectangles to each other, one after another as laid out, starting and finishing each seam 1cm (⅜in) from the edge, reversing at each end for strength. You should end up with one long piece, measuring 38 x 62cm (15 x 24½in).

3 With right sides together, stitch one of the squares to the top left-hand corner of your large piece, starting and finishing seam 1cm (⅜in) from the edge, and reversing for strength, as before.

4 Cut the thread and start a new line of stitching along the adjacent edge, in the same way as Step 3. Repeat on all four sides of the square until the piece of fabric made from rectangles is entirely attached along the four 17cm (6¾in) edges.

5 With right sides together, sew the two remaining long edges to each other, starting and stopping 1cm (⅜in) from each end, as before. You will now have a long rectangle shaped like a building block with the end missing.

6 Take your remaining square and, with right sides together, sew to the end of your 'building block' until only one side is left unsewn. Sew a little way along this seam from each end, leaving an opening in the middle.

7 Turn right side out through the opening and pop all eight corners out with your fingers, then fold your two remaining edges inside and stitch together. Your building block is complete.

8 Now push the square you have just sewn downwards to meet the bottom square, with the seams aligned, smoothing and folding the sides in half as you go so that they form the lining of your basket. Now use your fingers to press defined folds along the top rim of the basket.

9 Topstitch braid or decorative ribbon around the top edge of your basket. This is entirely optional, but it looks lovely and also helps to stiffen the rim a little.

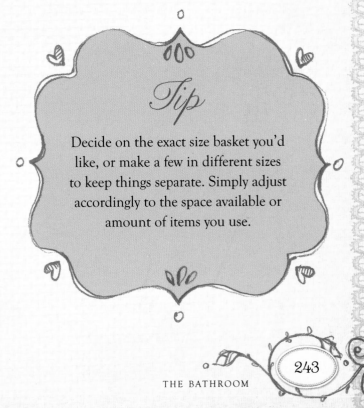

Tip

Decide on the exact size basket you'd like, or make a few in different sizes to keep things separate. Simply adjust accordingly to the space available or amount of items you use.

The world can wait
bath pillow

How I sometimes wish I could languish in the bath, reading fashion magazines or a novel the way I once did BC (Before Children). I would quite happily stay there for hours, loose-limbed in the near-boiling heat, deftly turning the tap every 15 minutes or so with my toes, topping up the water when it went cold and inhaling the lavender-scented steam. A whole afternoon could pass this way, when I was time-rich. It will not surprise you that my fingers became wrinkled as a crone (a necessary side-effect) and the only person I had to clean up after was myself (happy days indeed, if only in this respect).

Nowadays, I'm lucky for the chance to shower in peace, and our bath is so full of frightening sea creatures – and no doubt crawling with germs between cleans – adults don't often bathe in it at all.

Take opportunities when you can and escape to the bath with this plush pillow. It's very handy for avoiding a cricked neck, and should aid and abet your escape admirably (just be sure to discard any creatures with teeth ... plastic sharks, toddlers, etcetera).

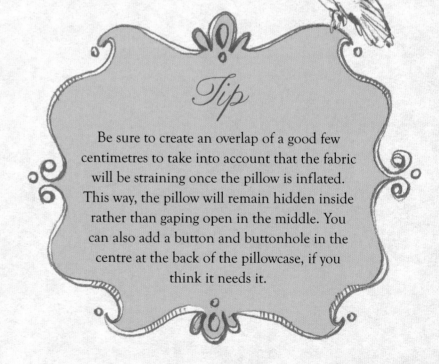

MATERIALS NEEDED

- Horseshoe-shaped blow-up travel pillow, available from a chemist or airport store
- Pretty floral cotton fabric
- Dressmaker's chalk
- Dressmaker's scissors
- Ruler
- Sewing machine and thread
- Pins
- Button (optional)

Tip

Be sure to create an overlap of a good few centimetres to take into account that the fabric will be straining once the pillow is inflated. This way, the pillow will remain hidden inside rather than gaping open in the middle. You can also add a button and buttonhole in the centre at the back of the pillowcase, if you think it needs it.

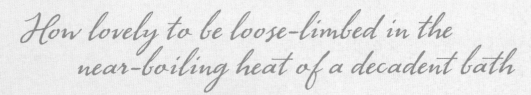

*How lovely to be loose-limbed in the
near-boiling heat of a decadent bath*

INSTRUCTIONS

1 Lay out your floral print fabric, right side down, and place the deflated travel pillow on top.

2 Use the chalk to draw around the outside of the pillow's shape.

3 Take your scissors and start cutting around the pattern created by the chalk, adding a few extra centimetres (an inch) the entire way around for your seam allowance. (Remember that the pillow will eventually be inflated, so be generous.) This is the front – set it aside.

4 Place the deflated pillow upon the fabric again, taking care not to waste too much fabric in between, but this time, draw only around the top half of the horseshoe, and halfway down its curving sides. Use the ruler to draw a straight line across the centre of the headrest.

5 Cut out the fabric, once again adding a few extra centimetres (an inch) the entire way around for your seam allowance.

6 Now place the deflated pillow upon the remaining fabric, this time drawing around the bottom half of the horseshoe and up its curving sides to take in just over half of the actual headrest, and use the ruler to draw a straight line again.

7 Cut this piece out as well, adding a few extra centimetres (an inch) the entire way around for your seam allowance. You should now have three pieces of fabric: the front and two overlapping backs.

8 Press under a narrow double hem on the raw straight edge of each of the overlapping backs and sew in a straight line across – you have just created hems for the opening.

9 Lay the front on your work surface, right side facing up, then place the two backs on top, right sides down, overlapping the hemmed edges until they are the same size as the front.

10 Use pins to secure the overlapping sides and back and front sections of fabric together, around the entire outer edge of the horseshoe shape.

11 Sew around the outer edge with your sewing machine.

12 Turn right side out through the lapped opening, poking out the edges with your fingers, and insert the inflatable pillow, before blowing it up to fill the pillow's new case.

246

THE ORIGIN OF THE BATH

The ancient Romans and Greeks certainly knew a thing or two about plumbing when communal bathing became a routine affair over 2,000 years ago. Strangely though, its popularity ceased during the Dark and Middle Ages. Unaware of the links between cleanliness and good health, the Great Unwashed died in large numbers from all sorts of viruses and contractible diseases, which might have been avoided with a good scrub. Like most good ideas, the art of bathing eventually resurfaced.

During the Regency period, bath houses began to thrive in spa towns around the UK. The Georgians were sold all sorts of health reasons for taking the plunge and, before long, worked out the link with personal hygiene. This led to a plethora of designs and materials becoming the latest thing in bathing: from the humble tin bath (which was later coated in enamel to prolong the experience and also looked quite nice), to cast iron, copper, and incredible achievements in marble and stone.

As plumbing became more widespread in Victorian times, the standalone bath, which had been put away after each use, gave way to the permanent fixture, with its very own room named after it. It was raised on legs, which in turn became highly ornamental. Styles such as claw-and-ball feet and the slipper or double slipper, sunken and so on, were most common. It is interesting to note that traditionally, bathing in the West is predominantly horizontal, however, in the Far East, baths are often vertical. This draws a parallel with the way the different cultures paint, write and read.

Fun fact: the word Jacuzzi is a tradename rather than a style, and was named after the company who first supplied the bits that made the hot tub bubble – it's doubtful the term would have been adopted if they hadn't had such a sassy name.

Très fabu
medicine cabinet

Switzerland is known for its orderliness, cuckoo clocks, chocolates and striking flag, depicting a white cross motif against solid red background. Maybe it was the Swiss Army knife I had as a child (a gender-specific subversion on behalf of my parents), or perhaps an embarrassing trait towards melodrama in illness, for I also have a penchant for medicine cabinets that find themselves emblazoned with the First Aid opposite of the distinctive Swiss flag – a red cross on a white background.

Mount one of these on your bathroom wall (preferably a second-hand, reclaimed version – there are many to be found in flea markets and the like) or give a boring wooden box a makeover with a coat of red paint and stencilled white cross – or vice versa.

MATERIALS NEEDED

- Reclaimed wooden box with opening door, lending itself to wall mounting or being used as a vintage bathroom cabinet
- Sandpaper and block
- Damp cloth
- Paper
- Ruler
- Pencil
- Craft knife
- Paint and paintbrush
- Masking tape
- Spray paint (optional)
- Crystal knob (optional)
- Drill
- Screws and plastic wall plugs

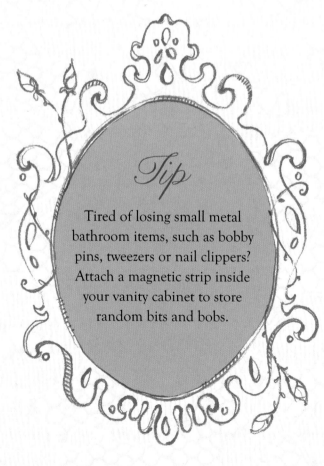

Tip

Tired of losing small metal bathroom items, such as bobby pins, tweezers or nail clippers? Attach a magnetic strip inside your vanity cabinet to store random bits and bobs.

248

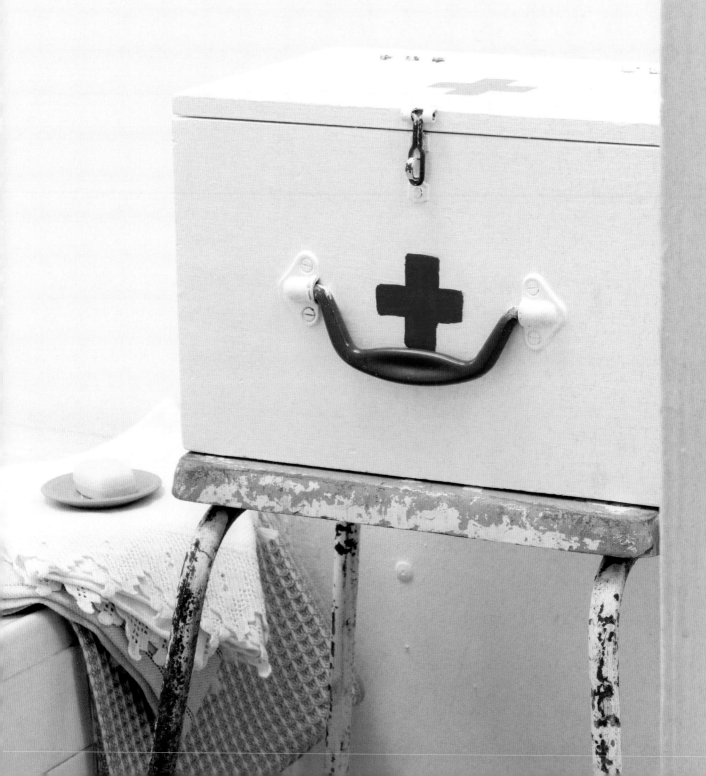

INSTRUCTIONS

1. Lightly rub your wooden box all over with the sandpaper, then remove any dust with a damp cloth.

2. Paint cabinet with chosen base shade of red or white. Allow first coat to dry fully before applying another.

3. With your ruler, pencil and paper, draw a Swiss-style cross to adorn your cabinet.

4. Cut out the shape with your craft knife, and place the stencil over the cabinet (when it has completely dried), lining up in the centre or wherever you wish the stencil to appear.

5. Secure stencil in place with masking tape.

6. Use paint or spray paint to fill in stencil, being careful not to spray or drip paint around or under the edges of the stencil.

7. If you wish to add or replace the knob, drill a hole to one side of the door, opposite the hinges, and screw to wood.

8. Work out where you wish the cabinet to sit, mark the spot with a pencil, and prepare to mount it on the bathroom wall.

9. Drill holes in the box first if none are already present, then place plastic wall plugs in the wall and affix the screws with the drill.

THE CRAFTY MINX *AT HOME*

THREE SHEETS TO THE WIND

Although the Georgians had a lot of time for Roman Baths, private bathing is a relatively new phenomenon. The individual bathroom was nowhere near as commonplace as it is today, which is why the simple towel rail – an integral bathing room accoutrement, designed to dry individual bath sheets in damp, draughty Victorian-era homes – was only created in the mid-19th century. As a single purpose piece of furniture, early towel rails were either attached to the wall or built as handsome, standalone pieces. Many examples of various designs and materials are in existence, from the plain, yet sturdy, timber standalones to be found in every country cottage, through to the decidedly more ornate metal versions, furnished with multiple sections and attachments for Madam's drying pleasure.

EARLY
TOWEL
RACKS

Tip

Repurpose brass railway luggage racks for a quirky addition to your modern bathroom. Available cheaply at auction houses, they make excellent storage for folded towels and echo the style of some of the smartest hotels in Europe, namely the high-design pedigree of the Hotel Costes chain in Paris and beyond.

Next to Godliness

LAUNDRY LOVE

The laundry is an oft-neglected area of the home, but one that can be so much more appealing and useful with some thoughtful investment. I'm not suggesting excessive spending to bring it up to scratch – you may already possess all the items you need to inject it with real character – but apply smarts, instead, to creating the perfect blend of utility and retro charm. If for no other reason than you won't begrudge spending countless hours there, muttering over the perennially refreshed piles of washing to be done.

Beg, borrow or buy unusual items fit for a crafty laundry overhaul. Pretty lengths of vintage fabric make a vast difference when employed in the form of new curtains, a fresh ironing board cover or wicker basket lining (go for a little nudge-nudge, wink-wink housewifely matching while you're at it) and seek out affordable vintage fixtures and fittings such as old ceramic basins or troughs, solid wooden cupboards and tarnished garden pots for storing bits and bobs. Let your look evolve over time.

Consider all manner of repurposed materials: anodised metal lampshades and furniture convey Industrial Chic, whereas medium-stained woods set against eggshell cream enamel say Country Cottage Comes to Town. Display starched white linen or stacks of fluffy bath sheets on open shelving, and ditch unlovely plastic buckets in favour of metal pots or '50s bread bins for overnight soaking. Store soaps and scrubbing brushes on various vintage saucers, tucking unsightly detergents away in cupboards or transferring their contents to a pretty tin or spray container. Keep a quaint feather duster out on display, and consider papering or stencilling the walls with classic motifs, such as fleur-de-lys or spriggy florals, to brighten up a tiny space.

In lieu of your own personal valet or maid, bite the bullet and create your very own laundry to love.

Beg, borrow or buy unusual items fit for a crafty laundry overhaul

Lovely lined
wicker basket

I quite like the countrified charm of a chintzy, girly laundry, especially in our super-modern times, where gleaming white surfaces rule the day and whitegoods are so overly engineered, they virtually run the home on their own, *Jetsons*-style.

Match your wicker basket to your ironing board cover to your peg bag, or be eclectic and mix them up for added interest when you're working your way through a mountain of washing. Hooray for hot summer days and a light, fresh breeze.

MATERIALS NEEDED

- Wicker washing basket
- Fabric, to line your basket – 1m (40in) should be enough, depending on its size and shape
- Dressmaker's chalk
- Dressmaker's scissors
- Sewing machine and thread
- 6mm- (¼in-) wide elastic
- Small safety pin

Indulge yourself with a chintzy, girly
laundry — all the better to wash in

INSTRUCTIONS

1. Take your fabric and lay it out beneath your basket, under its oval or rectangular base. Use chalk to draw outline and cut out, leaving a 2.5cm (1in) seam allowance, just in case. Make sure you use the fabric as sparingly as possible, cutting along the edges rather than from the middle.

2. Take the remaining strip of fabric and spread out inside the basket, making sure you have enough to cover the inside and then some – including an overlap on the upper edge – before cutting out the shape to fit the basket's interior.

3. With right sides facing each other, sew the edges of the sides together.

4. With right sides facing each other, pin the base piece to the lower edge of the upper section. If the lower edge seems to be too big to fit the base, run a gathering stitch around the edge and pull it up slightly to ease in the fullness. Distribute the gathers evenly, then stitch in place.

5. Press under 0.5cm (¼in) on the upper edge, then turn under another 1cm (³⁄₈in) and stitch close to the edge, creating a narrow casing. Leave a small opening to insert the elastic.

6. Use a safety pin to thread elastic through the casing and pull up until it fits over the edge of the basket, handles and all. Stitch the ends of the elastic together and sew up the opening. *Voilà*, you're done.

Tip

You can line virtually any storage container in the same way as this wicker basket. It provides a prettier look overall than simple utilitarian storage.

THE CRAFTY MINX AT HOME

Perfect press
ironing board cover

Vintage ironing boards can be a touch rickety and heavy, but look wonderfully authentic in the laundry. Old wooden versions require woolly batting to pad out any hard edges and cover splintery zones, and a good oiling for squeaky metal hinges every once in a while.

I've customised mine with a handmade cover constructed from a lovely Toile de Jouy fabric. Why not make ironing (such a bothersome exercise) more romantic with some refreshing eye candy?

MATERIALS NEEDED

- Pretty cotton fabric measuring approximately 50 x 135cm (20 x 53in) (enough to cover your ironing board, and then some)
- Extra scrap fabric to fit underneath if your ironing board has an unusual fin shape
- Dressmaker's scissors
- Bias binding
- Sewing machine and thread
- 5mm- (¼in-) wide elastic
- Small safety pin

INSTRUCTIONS

1 Lay your fabric out on the floor, right side down.

2 Turn your ironing board upside down and place it on top. Using the board's shape as a pattern, cut around the edge, giving yourself several centimetres' (a few inches') allowance around its outer edge, in order to allow for the overlap and casing.

3 Attach bias binding to the outer edge, on the wrong side, with your sewing machine.

4 When you reach the beginning again, cut off bias length leaving a space of about 2.5cm (1in).

5 Fold bias binding over to the right side and topstitch in place on the cover, close to the edge, making sure there's enough room for a small safety pin and elastic to pass through.

6 Finish by threading the elastic through the narrow casing, then pull it up to fit snuggly and secure the ends. Now pop it on top of your ironing board.

Tip

If your board has a weird fin shape at one end, like the one in the background here, you will need to create a pillowcase-style end by cutting another piece of fabric to cover underneath the fin shape, and sewing the two sections together before adding the bias binding casing.

A PRESSING MATTER

IRONING
ACCOUTREMENTS

Up until World War I, most household laundry was taken care of by washerwomen and under-footmen. The original iron was a flat iron or box iron, heated up on the fire or stovetop (or filled with hot coals) and applied directly to fabric or pressed over a thin ironing sheet to protect delicate pieces. These irons had triangular metal trivets that they sat in when not in use. There were tiny flat irons for intricate lacework, ranging up to much larger examples commonly used for clothing, curtains and sheets. The flat iron eventually gave way to the steam iron, and further evolved with the invention of electricity. Despite the changes wrought by technology, the basic triangular shape has stayed true over time.

Another household item which also hasn't changed much throughout history is the ironing board. Given its social stigma (being an entirely utilitarian and rather un-flashy piece of furniture), it's hardly surprising that, up until recently, nobody bothered trying to design anything new. Modern designers have played with slight variations on the form, although the basic construction (a board atop folded legs) remains.

Certainly popular in the collecting field, irons fare particularly well at auction, with collections of thousands or more snapped up by individual buyers over the course of a single afternoon. A common way to repurpose the flat iron is by putting it to use as a doorstop – the origin of many a stubbed toe.

Knickers in a twist
scanties bag

Who has time for handwashing? Pop your bras and undies in a wash bag instead, and run it through the delicates cycle on your washing machine with a gentle wool wash. It works a treat, and frees one from the drudgery of '50s housewifery.

Use this scanties bag for storing stockings and pantyhose on a hook inside the wardrobe, or run them through the machine inside this handy bag after wear.

MATERIALS NEEDED

- 38 x 78cm (15 x 31in) cotton or voile, such as this pretty, art deco-style Tana lawn print by Liberty of London
- Dressmaker's scissors
- Iron
- Ruler
- 80cm (31½in) woven cotton tape
- 80cm (31½in) colourfast cord or ribbon
- Small safety pin

INSTRUCTIONS

1 Fold fabric in half, wrong sides together (to measure 38 x 39cm (15 x 15½in), folded) and sew around the bottom and side edge, allowing 0.5cm (¼in) seam allowance. Leave the top edge open.

2 Use scissors to trim allowance close to the seam, and snip off corners at an angle.

3 Turn inside out, iron flat, and sew around the two sides again to create a French seam.

4 Fold under a narrow double hem on the raw edge of the opening and sew flat.

5 Measure 10cm (4in) down from the opening, then take your cotton tape and sew it around the inside of the bag, close to both tape edges, creating a casing. Neatly fold under the raw edges on each end of the tape to prevent fraying.

6 Turn bag right side out again and iron flat.

7 Unpick a few stitches in the side seam to gain access to the casing. Pop a safety pin on the end of your ribbon, and thread it through the cotton tape casing until you reach the hole again.

8 Pull through the ribbon, knot the ends together and pull the knot through until it is hidden in the casing.

La la land
lavender sachets

Oh, the granny connotations of a lavender sachet. But grannies understand how divinely scented soaps and sachets for the drawers are a pleasant reminder of the everyday joy of creature comforts. My Northern Italian ancestors probably left clothing hung in the branches of a mountain tree to air, living as they did on the side of a harsh alpine slope. I, on the other hand, have a chest full of vintage cashmere cardis and tiny lavender-filled pillows to transport me every time I go searching for something to wear. And it's much cosier in my house than on the side of a whopping great mountain, *capisce*? (They must, however, have been blessed with a better view.)

Sachets are a canny way to use small, pretty fabric scraps, handkerchiefs and tattered, cross-stitch-adorned linens. Backed with modern fabric, vintage scraps look more gorgeous than granny, more 'now' than nanna. Purchase the highest quality dried lavender to fill them, and dream a little dream of Provence every time you open your drawers.

MATERIALS NEEDED

- Two 12 x 12cm (5 x 5in) fabric squares; try mixing vintage with modern
- 10cm (4in) narrow satin ribbon, for the hanger loop
- Sewing machine and thread, or needle and thread
- Chopstick / knitting needle
- Iron
- Dried lavender, to fill

INSTRUCTIONS

1 You can use two 12cm (5in) square scraps of fabric to construct sachets with a finished size of 10cm (4in) square, or patchwork incy pieces together to create the initial 12cm (5in) squares.

2 Pop a loop of satin ribbon between the two pieces of fabric in one corner, right sides together, and temporarily secure with a pin; the loop should be tucked inside, with the raw ribbon edges poking out from one corner.

3 Sew around three and a half edges of the squares, removing the pin as you sew over the corner and secure the ribbon in place.

4 Turn right side out and use a chopstick to poke out the corners.

5 Turn under the raw edges on the opening, and iron entire sachet flat.

6 Spoon in lavender until almost full, then stitch the opening closed.

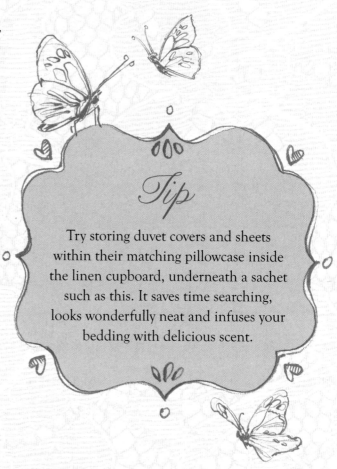

Tip

Try storing duvet covers and sheets within their matching pillowcase inside the linen cupboard, underneath a sachet such as this. It saves time searching, looks wonderfully neat and infuses your bedding with delicious scent.

Dream a little dream of Provence

Don't stop, Alfresco

ARTFUL OUTDOOR ROOMS

It wasn't until we considered selling our home recently that I finally had the back garden landscaped to be more useful, and guess what? It was one of the reasons we changed our minds about moving and decided not to sell. From the tiniest of roof gardens to sprawling wrap-around patios, and from postage stamp-sized inner city courtyards to luscious acres of gently rolling hills spied beyond the ha-ha, an outdoor room can be a mini kingdom for dining, relaxing and whiling away the hours in privacy or with the people you love, providing a valuable extension to your home.

Outdoor rooms are all about working with what you've got to create a fresh, open and sunny space to spend time: a quiet area to enjoy a novel or the newspaper, chat on the phone, relax with your thoughts or repair to with a laptop – multi-tasking work and the soaking up of some much-needed Vitamin D. Favourite plants and flowers offer cheery potted colour while releasing their oxygen and perfume into the air, and provide the perfect ingredients for a zen frame of mind, year-round. The other role of the outdoor room is as a backdrop for myriad celebrations: a space to shoot the breeze with family and friends, debut an untried dish for impromptu Sunday lunch, or watch the sun set over a cheeky cocktail or three. Set the mood with ornamental elements and tongue-in-cheek statements to show you're not like all the rest.

Outdoor areas are often decorated with hardier materials than those used indoors because they're exposed to the elements, but this doesn't mean outdoor living spaces need be devoid of personality. Stamp a handmade and vintage-inspired touch on gardens and alfresco dining areas in the form of bright fabrics, reclaimed furniture and sculptural displays. Amp up the quirk with plants stored in unusual pots, such as old zinc buckets or stone bowls, and weave special effects for specific events with paper decorations and custom-designed table settings.

For the best outdoor furniture, look to pew-style bench seats, wrought iron tables and chairs, and love seats placed to good advantage, as well as cane sofas and chaises longues. Be inventive, and consider the myriad possible uses for old crates and rusted metal sheeting. Birdbaths, stone pots and iron gates doubling as trellises look totally gorgeous, and wall decoration shouldn't be limited to indoors. Old metal advertising boards from the 1930s, '40s and '50s very effectively brighten up an outdoor space, and add a charming, original touch – all of which can be found in an easy trawl of the auction houses in your area on any given afternoon.

Think of your outdoor space as prime real estate, and address any neglect you've allowed to occur over time up until now – a veritable oasis may just be at your fingertips. Even if it never quite matches the Hanging Gardens of Babylon, it's well worth giving it a go.

Art deco
cane sofa and chairs

I've long admired the '20s look of bent cane chairs, which are so handsome set amongst a collection of ferns, cast in dappled, filtered light. Far more refined than most modern outdoor furniture, cane is redolent of cocktail hours spent on the croquet lawn, tennis whites, and lolling under slowly oscillating fans in a far-flung colonial outpost before the fall of the empire.

I bought this three-piece outdoor setting for the grand total of sixty dollars from a local flea market, and covered it with a fetching upholstery fabric from Publisher Textiles (for their details, see the supplier list on page 298). Originally a natural cane colour, it's been given a modern twist with black paint, lacquer and newly made cushions and backrests.

Old cane sofas and chairs are relatively easy to find for very little in second-hand stores and flea markets. Don't be put off by cosmetic damage: simply sand and lacquer, or paint over entirely if the cane is showing signs of age, but beware of rot and rickety joinery. Gnawed all over, my three-piece had obviously been chewed by the family dog. I simply sanded back the worst affected areas before giving these old *Grandes Dames* a much-needed makeover.

THE CRAFTY MINX *AT HOME*

*Cane: so redolent of cocktail hours
on the croquet lawn and tennis whites*

MATERIALS NEEDED

- Cane furniture
- Sandpaper and block
- Gloss paint and/or lacquer – 1l (1qt) of each will be plenty
- Two cushion inserts to fit each item: you may need to have these custom-made. For this project, I took my cushion specifications to a local foam and rubber manufacturer, who made them up for me. My base cushions are three-dimensional, but we're going to make a two-dimensional cushion cover rather than attempt to make boxed covers to fit perfectly (see the instructions on how to do this on page 276)
- Upholstery fabric to fit both front and back. Remember that you need to allow extra fabric so that the covers can be folded to accommodate the box shape of your cushions. You can use the same fabric on top and bottom, or save money by using top quality fabric on one side and matching canvas or denim underneath – allow a little more fabric for the backing, as this is where the zippers will be inserted and more is needed in the seams
- One zipper for each cushion, roughly 65cm (25in) long
- Ruler
- Dressmaker's chalk
- Dressmaker's scissors or pinking shears
- Sewing machine and thread
- Denim needle for sewing machine
- Needle and thread

REVITALISING CANE FURNITURE

When buying second-hand cane for a bargain, chances are it will be showing signs of age, having being left outside in the elements. The choice is up to you whether to paint over or sand back and re-lacquer. I've painted mine entirely in black, with a topcoat of lacquer – this best matches my cushion fabric, but natural cane looks gorgeous also with complementary designs. A bright paint job also works to convey a cheery, modern feel.

Sand the cane back with sandpaper and a block. Dust off with a brush or damp cloth. Apply two coats of paint and two coats of lacquer, allowing adequate drying time between each application.

INSTRUCTIONS FOR CONSTRUCTING CUSHIONS

1 From the fabric for the cushion front, cut a 73cm (29in) square. (This measurement will, of course, depend on the size of your own cushion insert.)

2 Measure and cut your backing fabric into two pieces: for mine, I've made one 73 x 14.5cm (29 x 5¾in) and the other 73 x 61.5cm (29 x 24¼in).

3 With right sides together, align the two backing pieces along the 73cm (29in) edge.

4 Take your zip and lay it along this 73cm (29in) edge so that it is equidistant from both ends. Make a mark on the edges of the fabric to show where the zip opening should start and finish.

5 Put the zip aside and, allowing a 1.5cm (½in) seam, sew the seam closed at each end, from your mark to the edge, leaving the seam open in the middle. Press the seam allowance open, pressing open the edges of the unstitched section as well.

6 With the right side of the fabric facing upwards, position your closed zip under the opening (make sure it's facing up the right way) and pin it in place. Pin one folded edge of the opening about 2mm (⅛in) from the zipper teeth and then pin the other side, about 1cm (⅜in) from the folded edge. Place a pin across the seam at the top and bottom of the opening, one pin just above the pull tab and the other just below the zip stop. It is a good idea to tack the zip in position now before stitching it, as the pins can get a bit awkward while you stitch.

7 Using a zipper foot on your machine, sew the zip in place, stitching along both sides and pivoting on the needle at the corners to stitch across the top and bottom too.

8 You should now have a cushion back that measures 73cm (29in) square.

9 Open the zip about 2–3cm (⅛–¼in). With right sides together, raw edges matching and allowing a 1.5cm (½in) seam, stitch the cushion front to the back around all edges.

10 Snip diagonally across each corner to remove the extra fabric – take care not to cut into your stitching – and turn the cover right side out through the zip opening. Push the corners out with your fingers.

11 Insert the cushion pad into your cover and zip it up.

12 Take your needle and thread, fold down the excess fabric at the edges as though you were wrapping a present, and sew a few tacking stitches into place, thus creating a box-shaped cover. This is far easier than creating covers to fit three-dimensional cushions, and only needs to be unpicked and re-stitched once a year or so when washing.

THE CRAFTY MINX AT HOME

A POTTED HISTORY

In 18th-century Britain, people with taste or money did the 'Grand Tour', enjoying and seeking inspiration in the capital cities of Europe. The neo-classical style of the period (with its classic proportions, scale and architectural motifs) is firmly embedded as the epitome of Georgian design, and a good deal of furniture and decorative items were produced during this period. With the rise in popularity of landscape gardeners such as Capability Brown, and the trend towards formal gardens becoming an extension of any stately home, the style lent itself well to geometric garden designs featuring decorative sculptural pieces.

Arthur Wellesley, the Duke of Wellington, was passionate about collecting, and inspired fellow countrymen following the Grand Tour craze to return with souvenirs such as the Elgin Marbles. Obviously, not everyone could afford the time or money to make the Tour and bring back such weighty items, so a burgeoning market developed for homegrown pieces that copied the styles of the day. Coadestone (named after its inventor, Eleanor Coade) was introduced around the 1800s and was used often throughout this period to create garden accoutrements. An artificial cement stone, cast and fired at high temperatures rather than sculpted to resemble marble, it turned out to cost more to produce than carved marble and was therefore abandoned. It is seldom seen today.

The main design motifs associated with this period are geometrical columns, pilasters and architraves, and softer motifs such as swags, husks, egg-and-dart borders, cornucopiaes and the naked human form. 'After the Antique' urns and trophy-shaped pots were also very popular, all of which still heavily influence decorative parterre (formal garden) pieces today.

Very tinkly indeed …

Off-key wind chime mobile

Rope your favourite little one in to help with this one – it beats an afternoon parked in front of the telly and finds an inspired use for found objects and various bits and bobs. I love the sound these old crystal chandelier pieces and keys make in the wind. Very tinkly indeed.

MATERIALS NEEDED

- Two sticks – set off on an adventure to the park to find these
- Ribbon or string
- Various found objects made of metal, such as keys, nails or screws
- Reclaimed chandelier pieces or other found objects such as shells and stones
- Fishing line

INSTRUCTIONS

1. Take your two sticks and cross each over the other, wrapping ribbon or string around the middle section to secure, before tying in a bow.

2. Tie the fishing line to your metal objects, and start hanging each near the other, testing the sounds they make by tapping together as you tie each one on to a new section of the crossed sticks. You want to aim for a soft tinkling sound when the wind blows.

3. Add other found objects in the same way, wrapping and knotting fishing line over each item before hanging for attractive effect.

4. Tie a length of string or more fishing line around the middle of the crossed sticks, and hang from a branch or undercover awning. Wait for a gust and, hey presto, is that the chime?

*The use of unusual pots
and planters showcases a
riotous collection of green*

Planters to please

Just about the best home garden I ever saw wasn't really a garden at all, but a London roof terrace, measuring no more than 4 x 4m (4 x 4yd) and edged on all four sides by planter boxes overflowing with a wild selection of small trees, flowers and shrubs, and unconventional pots stacked upon every available surface. With a tiny zone left free in the middle for outdoor dining, it was compact, charming and ever-so-suited to its owner's need for an additional entertaining area and city escape-hatch; much like the gardens spied on the roofs of houseboats in Amsterdam's canals. Although it was a brilliantly clever use of space and peaceful sanctuary from the capital's bustling, overcrowded streets, what I admired most about this terrace garden was the use of unusual pots and planters to showcase a riotous collection of green.

Old fruit boxes and packing crates, leaky zinc buckets, ceramic bowls, empty tin cans and even hollow statues with the tops lopped off provide an unpredictable alternative to the traditional terracotta or black plastic pot. Not just for city folk, these unusual planters look great in country gardens too. Experiment with a range of hardy vessels, drilling holes into the base for adequate drainage and stacking in a wire or metal frame to protect from being knocked over in a stiff wind.

A flowering lemon or magnolia tree looks particularly magic in this setting – try an old tin drum or wooden tea chest stacked on a base of reclaimed bricks, and recline on a deck chair to admire the fruits of such thrifty labour.

Bluebird of happiness bird feeder

There are myriad uses for old china tea saucers and plates, which can be found in almost every charity store and local flea market across the country. Doubling as drainage stands for pot plants, soap dishes, jewellery trays and dip bowls, now you can add this pretty bird feeder to the list.

Made from a salvaged vintage plate – once part of a teacup and saucer trio – and a wire coathanger, this feeder looks sweet hung outside a kitchen window or in the garden. Add birdseed and watch the local avian population flock to your home. Children, in particular, will love to see them alight and feed, so ask for 'help' creating this simple craft project together.

MATERIALS NEEDED

- Vintage plate – opt for a chintzy floral or English countryside motif
- About 80cm (30in) firm tie wire
- Wire cutters
- Pliers
- Glue gun and glue
- Pearl embroidery thread or fishing line (embroidery thread adds colour, but fishing line will be hardier for long-term use in the outdoor elements)
- Christmas tree decoration or other found decorative objects
- Twine
- Birdseed

INSTRUCTIONS

1 Take your length of wire and bend it gently into a bell jar-like shape, as shown in the photograph.

2 Use the pliers to bend over the ends of the wire by approximately 1cm (³⁄₈ in) each, creating small hooks that will fit snugly under the edges of your plate.

3 Hook the folded ends into place underneath the plate base and use pliers to fold the wire back sharply over the edges, crimping the wire around the plate edge until secured into place.

4 Heat up glue gun and pop a few spots of hot glue under each side of the plate between plate and tie wire – this will secure base to the wire and prevent it from slipping out.

5 Wrap fishing line or pearl embroidery thread around the top of the feeder and tie decorative objects on, such as this tin bird decoration or white china bird. Ask the little people in your home for help at this stage of the feeder's construction.

6 Tie a length of twine to the top of the feeder, and hang from a tree branch or window awning.

7 Place birdseed on vintage plate base, and wait for the local birds to twig to their new food source. Experiment with different varieties if you don't see any action in the first few days.

Tip

A couple of these cute bird feeders hung together at different levels look simply gorgeous as a fantasy feature in a child's bedroom, and take no time to complete. They also look charming in the garden, but if you are actually going to use them as bird feeders, remove the twinkling decorations, as they tend to frighten little feathered friends away.

THE CRAFTY MINX AT HOME

Trip the stripes fantastic
bench seat

Anything as colourful as this brightly coloured bench seat tends to put a smile on the face, *non*? The glossy stripes remind me of summer holidays, beach towels and lazy days spent lolling about in a deck chair. Have a bunch of friends around and invite them to pull up a pew. Mojitos optional.

MATERIALS NEEDED

- Vintage bench seat from a flea market or second-hand store
- Filler
- Sandpaper and block
- Damp cloth
- Undercoat paint
- Ruler
- Pencil
- Various gorgeous paint shades in high-gloss acrylic
- Low-tack masking tape
- Paintbrush

INSTRUCTIONS

1. Firstly, use filler to stop up any gaps in wood joins, fill empty nail holes and generally smooth out rough surfaces.

2. Once the filler is dry, rub with sandpaper to remove any excess and remove dust with a damp cloth, ready for your undercoat.

3. Apply a layer of undercoat with paintbrush, and allow to dry completely. Now you're ready for the fun part.

4. Use a ruler, pencil and masking tape to demarcate stripes along the length of the bench seat, making sure your stripes are the correct width apart on either side and wrapping tape over each edge and down legs if required.

5. Paint a new colour in random stripe widths along the seat. This looks deliciously brilliant – just like deckchair fabric. Apply three coats for a gorgeous, glossy finish.

6. Once paint is fully dry (wait at least 24 hours), remove the first set of masking tape stripes and add more over the already-painted stripes at the edges.

7. Fill in white spaces with three coats of paint and allow to fully dry.

8. Remove masking tape and admire your gorgeous pew.

Tip

Choose your paint colours by taking fabric or paper clippings of your favourite shades to the store with you, and have them mixed up for the closest match. Don't bother buying entire pots – small tester-sized pots for each colour should provide enough to finish an entire seat or two.

Epilogue

There is so much joy to be found in making a home and, in particular, a home filled with beloved, vintage and handmade objects. Constantly re-ordering, re-sorting and re-using things to reflect your moods and style inspirations can become a life's work that never ends, especially when you consider that the pieces you treasure now will probably be incorporated into another space one day, whether handed down as heirlooms or salvaged from your unwanted belongings when you move on and evolve. Rather than being attached to belongings like a hoarder, see yourself as their guardian for a time, and take on this role with care and consideration.

Building an inspirational home is something I think goes hand-in-hand with being a grown-up. There's something completely delicious in knowing that I alone am responsible for my environment and how it nurtures both me and my loved ones. It's totally unique to us, and reflects where we've been and where we're going. This is why I always strive to keep it fresh and out of stasis. Perhaps it's the restlessness of my childhood and teenage years as well as my twenties, where I moved often and to various cities, in search of a real home before returning to Sydney where I grew up and now live. Now I own a home of my own, I cherish it dearly, but it's so much more than having a mortgage that connects me to the place. It's the energy I've invested to create a family home we can love living in for the foreseeable future.

Thrifting vintage objects for upcycling and crafting from scratch is all about being open to inspiration wherever you find it, and taking time out to enjoy the tactile and true pleasure of making things by hand. It's about not discarding things in a fit of carelessness or frustration, but really thinking about how you can make something work in another context, repairing it or finding an appropriate home for it elsewhere when all else fails.

As with everything in life, be adventurous and bold when it comes to feathering your nest and you'll be rewarded with the kinds of experiences and belongings that make for great company during the advancing years. Be proud of who you are and how your home reflects this, and have fun. Don't take yourself and the notion of style too seriously; it's been said before and I'll say it again – life's simply too short for such worries.

The tactile and true
pleasure of making things
by hand never grows old

Useful Equipment & Materials

Start small when it comes to buying equipment, rather than stocking up on costly items you might never use. Very few of these are absolutely essential, but here's a list of the things I find most useful. Acquire them as needed for different projects:

TOOLS & HARDWARE

- Craft knife and spare blades
- Staple gun and staples
- Hammer
- Nails in different sizes
- Screws and eye hooks
- Pliers and wire cutters
- Power drill with a variety of drill-bit sizes
- Wood saw
- Sandpaper and block
- Ruler and set square
- Glue gun and extra glue sticks
- Craft glue
- Tacky craft glue
- Decoupage glue
- Spray adhesive
- Roller cutter and cutting mat (for art mounting; do not use your fabric cutter)
- Paper scissors
- Mounting board in neutral shades such as black or off-white
- A selection of paintbrushes
- Masking tape (and low-tack masking tape)

- Screen for screen-printing
- Squeegee
- Water-soluble screen-printing ink
- Rubber roller (if you plan to do lots of decoupage)
- Lacquer or varnish
- Beeswax
- WD40 (for rust)
- Tie wire

SEWING THINGS

- Sewing machine
- Machine needles: standard, denim and delicate (for silk and organza)
- Bobbins and bobbin case
- Sidewinder (this is a separate bobbin winder – you can wind bobbins on your machine so you don't really need it, but they come in handy when you're using your machine a lot. I bought my first sidewinder a year ago.)
- Tape measure
- Bobble-headed pins
- Fine sewing needles
- Safety pins
- Vliesofix or double-sided appliqué webbing

- A thimble (especially for quilting, leatherwork or when stitching through heavy fabrics to avoid painful blisters)
- Plastic yoyo makers in a variety of sizes
- Pompom makers (again, in a variety of sizes)
- Crochet hooks
- Larger embroidery / tapestry needles
- Dressmaker's scissors – a good pair should last a lifetime or longer, so buy the best you can afford and sharpen regularly
- Small, sharp scissors for loose threads
- Pinking shears (scissors with a zigzag edge) – good for cutting fabrics that fray easily, such as canvas or linen. Also useful to own a cheap pair specifically for cutting paper; the edge looks great on handmade cards, but don't mix them up or your fabric pair will be blunt in no time.
- Dressmaker's chalk
- Polyester or wool batting
- Quick Unpick / seam ripper
- Rotary cutter and cutting mat
- Quilter's rule
- Iron

Glossary of Basic Skills & Stitches

Backstitch

This simple embroidery stitch is worked in an unbroken line, so is useful for outlining shapes and for tracing over lettering. Bring your needle to the front of the fabric and take a small stitch backwards. Bring it up again, in front of the stitch you just worked, and insert the needle back into the starting point of the previous stitch. Continue in this way, working each subsequent stitch back towards the previous one, creating a continuous line of stitching.

Casing

A wide double hem that is used to thread ribbon or elastic through.

Clip across the corner

When you sew around a 90-degree corner, such as on a cushion cover, before turning the piece right side out, trim diagonally across each corner, close to the stitching. This reduces the bulk of fabric in the corner so that when you turn the piece right side out, your corners form neat points.

Clip the curves

When you sew a seam around a curve, before you turn the item right side out, carefully make small snips across the seam allowance towards your stitching. Take great care not to actually snip into the stitching itself. Make these snips at 1–2cm (³⁄₈–³⁄₄ in) intervals. When you turn the item right side out, the curved seam will sit nice and flat, without puckers.

Double hem

Turn the raw edge of your fabric to the wrong side – an iron is handy for doing this – then turn under the folded edge again and stitch along the inner edge. This creates a neat hem that completely encloses the raw edge.

Double-sided appliqué webbing

A wonderful adhesive-backed paper that enables you to cut and adhere appliqué shapes to fabric. It also seals the raw edges of the shapes, making fraying less of a problem. The only thing you need to remember is that the finished shapes will be mirror-images of the way they were traced – so if you're using letters, you need to trace them back to front.

French seam

This seam is stitched in two stages. First, lay your pieces of fabric together with the wrong sides facing each other. Stitch a narrow seam around the edges. Now turn the piece inside out, so the right sides are now facing each other. Use your iron to press the seamed edges nice and flat. Stitch around the edges again, allowing a slightly wider seam allowance than before. Turn the item right side out and press again. A French seam totally encloses the raw edges of your fabric so that no fraying can occur. It is ideal for delicate fabrics, those that fray badly or for items that need frequent washing.

Interfacing

A woven or non-woven fabric that is used to reinforce fabric, giving it more strength or body. It comes in a variety of thicknesses and is also available in a fusible version, which is ironed in place on the wrong side of your fabric.

THE CRAFTY MINX AT HOME

Machine-baste

Change the stitch length on your machine to the longest stitch available and stitch pieces together to hold them until you do the final stitching. It's the same as tacking by hand.

Mitre the edges

When you are folding fabric, paper or binding around a corner, you will have too much material at the corner itself. You need to fold the excess in such a way that you enclose it in neat folds. For paper, this might mean folding it as though you were wrapping a present; for fabric and binding, there are various ways of mitring, depending upon your project. The easiest way to learn to mitre edges or corners is to look for tutorials on the internet – there's nothing like your own private lesson.

Reverse at each end

When you sew a seam on the machine, you need to secure the threads so that the seam does not unravel. You can do this by reversing back and forth at each end of the seam. You can also pull the bobbin thread through to the front and tie off both threads by hand.

Right sides together

Place your pieces together so that the outside or patterned sides are facing inwards towards each other, and the wrong sides are facing out.

Running stitch

The simplest of all embroidery/sewing stitches. Using a needle and thread, take a series of small (or sometimes large), evenly sized stitches, one after the other in a linear direction, with an equal amount of space between each stitch. Traditional quilting stitch is also a series of very small running stitches, worked through all three layers of a quilt.

Satin stitch

A useful embroidery stitch for filling in small shapes and outlines. Bring your needle to the front at one side of the shape, then take the thread across the shape and insert the needle in the outline on the opposite side, taking care not to pull it too tightly. Bring it to the front again, very close to the previous stitch, and continue in this way, making a series of stitches across the shape to be filled, keeping your stitches straight and close together, and varying the width as the outline changes.

Seam allowance

The measurement that you need to add to the edges of your fabric when cutting to allow for stitching the seams. It can vary from 5mm to 2cm ($\frac{1}{4}$ to $\frac{3}{4}$in), depending on the fabric itself and the nature of your project. You do not need to add seam allowance to edges that will be finished with bias binding.

Topstitch

A line of stitching done on the right side of the fabric. It can be used to attach pieces during construction, as well as decoratively and to add strength to seams and edges.

Zipper foot

A special narrow foot for your sewing machine that allows you to sew close to the edge of the zipper teeth.

List of Suppliers

Following is a list of my favourite Australian suppliers, including the places I bought most of the fabric, vintage pieces and trimmings to produce all the projects in this book. These local businesses and marketplaces consistently create and sell beautifully produced items, which I find a pleasure to use, but they also fit the bill in terms of buying local and buying handmade, something I place a good deal of importance upon. I've included them here just in case you'd like to use the same or similar materials in your own projects and because, with the advent of web shopping, buying online is a possibility no matter where in the world you live.

Bear in mind the same sorts of businesses, run by equally passionate and creative people, are usually always located nearby no matter where you are – you just need to take the time and patience to find them.

Amazing Paper

For imported Japanese origami, rice and mulberry papers, and all papers and equipment for creating handmade cards, invitations and stylish scrapbooking

184 Enmore Road
Enmore NSW 2042
+61 2 9519 8237

www.amazingpaper.com.au

Calico & Ivy Haberdashery

Inspiring and knowledgeable team of craft experts stocking lovely yarns and Liberty fabrics as well as vintage-inspired fabric, useful crafting equipment and finished homewares. Also runs excellent craft workshops

10 Birchgrove Road
Balmain NSW 2041
+61 2 9555 9909

10 Glyde Street
Mosman Park WA 6012
+61 8 9383 3794

www.calicoandivy.com

Cloth Fabric

Beautiful hand-printed linens for upholstery
and quilting by designer Julie Paterson.
Also runs craft workshops

1/113–115 William Street
Darlinghurst NSW 2010
+61 2 9699 2266

www.clothfabric.com

EM Greenfield

Ribbons, trims and all manner of fabrics, feathers
and sequinned additions at wholesale prices

30–36 Ann Street
Surry Hills NSW 2010
+61 2 9212 1944

www.emgreenfield.com

Jodi McGregor Florists

Florals, moss and beautifully made homewares,
chosen by the award-winning florist herself

123 Johnston Street
Annandale NSW 2038
+61 2 9566 1999

www.jodie.com.au

Lawson's Auction House

Australia's premier auctioneers since 1884 and
an excellent source of quality vintage furniture,
art and bric-a-brac

1A The Crescent
Annandale NSW 2038
+61 2 9566 2377

www.lawsons.com.au

Me Too Please

Interesting, unique and ethically sourced Mexican
oilcloth and gifts

2–4 Nelson Street
Annandale NSW 2038
+61 2 9519 2398

www.metooplease.com.au

Mitchell Road Antique & Design Centre

More than 70 brilliant stalls stocking vintage
furniture, fabric, clothing and bric-a-brac

76 Mitchell Road
Alexandria NSW 2015
+61 2 9698 0907

www.mitchellroad.wordpress.com

Porter's Paints

Premium paints with no nasty fumes and stockists of a divine range of wallpapers and rare finishes such as milk paint and lime wash. Also runs workshops

Locations all across Asia-Pacific
1800 656 664

www.porterspaints.com

Publisher Textiles

Quirky and diverse hand-printed textiles and wallpaper by designer Mark Cawood

Unit 1/87 Moore Street
Leichhardt NSW 2040
+61 2 9569 6044

www.publishertextiles.com.au

Rozelle Markets

Sydney's best flea market, since 1991

663 Darling Street
Rozelle NSW 2039
+61 2 9818 5373

www.rozellemarkets.com.au

Signature Prints

For all Florence Broadhurst fabrics, wallpaper and unique homewares items

1–5 Hayes Road
Rosebery NSW 2018
+61 2 8338 8400

www.signatureprints.com.au

The Sydney Antique Centre

Australia's oldest antique centre with 50+ antiques and art dealers. Source of a wonderful range of vintage furniture, fashion, porcelain, glass, jewellery, clocks, kitchenware, lighting, Orientalia, rugs, sports memorabilia, bottles, books and all other collectables

531 South Dowling Street
Surry Hills NSW 2010
+61 2 9361 3244

www.sydantcent.com.au

Vinnies

Brilliant charity organisation doing good works across the country and stocking excellent second-hand clothes, furniture, books and bric-a-brac in their stores

Locations all across Australia

www.vinnies.org.au

THE CRAFTY MINX AT HOME

Acknowledgements

There are few things sweeter in life than doing a job you love, with people you respect.

To Diana Hill: our pitch went through several incarnations and you expertly nurtured it from a seed of an idea to a fully formed concept. Thank you for the layers, clever lady.

Thank you to my dear friend and publisher Catherine Milne for introducing me to HarperCollins and for your (at times unfounded) faith in my abilities. It seems right to be channelling a stadium anthem here: You're the Best.

Designer Jane Waterhouse and project editor Chren Byng, it's been an absolute pleasure. Thanks for listening, and honing your perfectionism in these pages – it shows. I hope we have the chance to do it all over again.

Photographer Amanda Prior and stylist Claire Delmar: two super-talented superwomen I feel blessed to have wrangled onto this team; what you achieved in five days was no small feat. I salute you!

Georgina Bitcon and Mary Keep, thank you for taking on the editing and proofreading at such short notice, and for simply making it better. I'm so grateful for your wealth of knowledge and talent.

Shauna Farren-Price, thanks for your foreword, friendship, and all the atmospheric bits and bobs, always. In another life, I wish I had your job.

To the lovely Kristy Allen: I can't imagine this book without your illustrations. We've been through the trenches together, and yet I'd do it all again, TM. Thanks heaps for going above and beyond.

Thanks to Varuna, the Writers' House, for providing a much-needed space to finish my manuscript. Thanks also to the writers I met staying there.

For many and varied reasons, thanks to: Katrina Collett, Olivier Dupon and Mark Wilsher, all the Doust and Jenkins clans, the Edmonds, the F-Ps, Steven Foulkes and Christine Curry, Jess Guthrie, Maggie Hamilton, Rebecca Huntley, Lou Johnson, Natasha Milne, April Murdoch, Sonia Palmisano and Michael Davis, Jacinta Tynan, Sarah Wheatley, and Dean Wilmot and Jacqueline Grima. Best support group ever.

To my funny, clever Olive: thanks for being you. And to my husband, James, who makes everything possible. GSOH doesn't cover it (you're also super-hot). Love love.

There is so much joy to be found in making a home ...

Praise for *The Crafty Minx*

'*The Crafty Minx* offers cute and playful craft ideas for all seasons, with an emphasis upon creative upcycling and gift-giving... this'll keep you busy without stressing you out with complicated instructions and long-winded projects destined to be chucked on the 'abandoned crafts' pile. Two thumbs up!'
– *Frankie* magazine

'Doust's clever book is written for those who need a little help mastering a needle and thread but still love the idea of making their own craftwork.'
– *Inside Out* magazine

'Like a cupcake: sweet, light and more-ish.'
– *Next* magazine

'Blogger, sewer extraordinaire and all-round crafty lady Kelly Doust has been making handmade treasures out of vintage fabrics and recycled wares since she was a girl. Now this bowerbird has compiled all her favourite projects in a bright, easy-to-follow book that encourages even the most creatively challenged to pick up a needle and thread.'
– *Home Beautiful* magazine

'I can't decide what I love the most in the book, except I LOVE IT ALL. But the cutest of all is the eye patch. Oh, and the tea cosy. Too gorgeous.'
– Rachel Castle, artist and homewares designer, Castle & Things

Praise for *Minxy Vintage*

'Kelly Doust introduces readers to her wonderful world of reviving and customising vintage pieces, with tips on how to find, buy, clean, repair and salvage vintage clothing. *Minxy Vintage* is a great guide for anyone who wants to bring their crafting and sewing skills to create personal and individual pieces from budget vintage finds, while bringing a modern and unique twist to wearing vintage clothes.'
– Dita Von Teese

'Kelly Doust is a girl after my own heart, reinventing vintage finds to suit her personal style. Her book is a vintage vixen's guidebook for the chic: just read, shop, recreate, and repeat. Her finds are exquisite and her reinvention tricks are inspiring and achievable for even the newest vintage shopper among us. You can't help but get inspired by her vintage acumen.'
– Janie Bryant, award-winning costume designer, *Mad Men*

'From customising op-shop pieces to putting a modern spin on retro designs, *Minxy Vintage* shows you how to breathe new life into preloved pieces. It's cute, creative and full of fun ideas.'
– *Marie Claire* magazine

'Paying as much attention to practicality and resourcefulness as it does to the current fashionable sensibility and aesthetics, Doust has fashioned a stylish addition to the ranks of books for Austerity Britain.'
– welovethisbook.com